Village Display Tips

E-Book #3

Stylistic Village Vignettes

by Leigh Gieringer & Sue Chretien

Creative ideas and tips to enhance your village displays & save space, too!

Published by

Leigh Gieringer Graphic Services
Chandler, AZ 85248

ISBN: 1-4910735-4-3
Library of Congress Number: 98-093227

The purpose of this book is to educate and provide ideas to collectors of lighted villages to further enhance their enjoyment in displaying their collections. Some ideas and photographs have been presented from other collectors and so credited. Any photo not otherwise identified was provided by Leigh Gieringer. The author and publisher shall have neither liability, nor responsibility to any person or entity with respect to implementation of these ideas.

This publication is not affiliated with Department 56, Inc. or any of its affiliates, subsidiaries, distributors or representatives. Department 56, Inc., The Original Snow Village, Snow Village Halloween, The Heritage Village Collection, The Dickens' Village Series, The New England Village Series, and the Christmas in the City Series are Trademarks of Department 56, Inc. Eden Prairie, Minnesota. The Alpine Village Series, The North Pole Series, The Little Town of Bethlehem Series are the copyright of Department 56, Inc. The Disney Village Series was a joint venture by both the Walt Disney Company®, and Department 56, Inc. Product names and product designs are the property of Department 56, Inc. The lighted buildings and accessories incorporated in the photos were used solely to illustrate display ideas, techniques and tips. Leigh Gieringer Graphic Services is not affiliated with any company whose products may appear in this book.

Table of Contents

Display on the cover: Leigh Gieringer
Display above: Sue Chretien (Page 100)
Displays on the back cover - top to bottom:
John Michael Sanders, Mark de Vries,
and Randy Vollett

PREFACE:

Collecting miniature village pieces is different from just about all other collectibles. Villaging has always been a unique and intriguing hobby. In years past, collectors typically did not acquired pieces to be put inside a curio cabinet or placed on a book self. They created realistic miniature settings around their favorite villages or pieces, or incorporated them into large mini metropolis' that they could enjoy and share with others. New introductions were obtained as soon as their dealers received them. Collectors had to have every piece associated with their village. But, village collecting is also fluid. It has the ability to change with tastes, life experiences, needs and limitations of the collector.

Today, many collectors are being more selective in their acquisitions because of cost and space considerations. Many of those collectors who have been adding to their collections since they were first introduced are finding that they do not have the time, space or energy to create mega displays any more, yet still wish to enjoy their favorite pieces. Many requests have been received to provide simple ideas that can be assembled in a short amount of time and not take up too much room.

*Therefore, a request for ideas to be included in a book featuring vignettes was published in an issue of the Village D-Lights magazine in late 2012. The response was fantastic, almost overwhelming. Enough material was provided to fill two books. **Realistic Village Vignettes**: Volume I of the Vignette Series provides numerous ideas to create vignettes in realistic settings. These ideas and techniques can be created as stand alone vignettes, or become focal points in much larger displays. **Stylistic Village Vignettes**: Volume II of the Vignette Series emphasizes stylistic approaches – those that are set into a container, themed with non-village items, paired with other collectibles, etc. Collectors can still treasure a favorite village piece in much smaller spaces, and merge them with other very special items to continue their enjoyment of the hobby.*

*The displays featured in the **Realistic Village Vignettes** and **Stylistic Village Vignettes** books can be used as creative inspiration to create your own small vignettes. There's a treasure trove in both books that will launch your creativity! Showcase your favorite buildings for holiday displaying or for year around enjoyment.*

Introduction

Do you know anyone who as ever said this?

"I love my miniature village! But, now I need/want (pick one) to downsize. I only have space to display just a few village pieces. I don't have the time to develop a large display. I want to do something different, or all of the above."

For people who have down-sized and can no longer do a complete village display, or want to do something different than they have done in past years, or simply want a unique and interesting way to showcase a special piece, you are going to love the *Village Vignettes Series* of display ideas. Lack of time and space has become a major challenge to really enjoying collections many have lovingly accumulated throughout the past years, even decades. Thus, collectors are seeking a different solution to feature their porcelain or ceramic buildings. Many have asked for new ideas to showcase select pieces or place in smaller areas. Others have been willing to share them.

Volume I of the *Village Vignette Series - **Realistic Village Vignettes** -* is based on realism - a building or series of buildings placed in a setting representing an actual scene. The second book in the *Village Vignette Series - **Stylistic Village Vignettes** -* takes a different direction. Instead of recreating a logical village in miniature, Sue Chretien, a master in developing unique stylized vignettes, artfully selects non-village items and couples them with her favorite buildings providing striking results. I've invited her to share several of her creative vignettes since it will help other collectors to further enjoy their village pieces on a smaller scale. Numerous other collectors have also provided wonderful ideas for showcasing their favorite pieces accented with non-village elements.

Always a focal point, some village pieces are

Page 6

Page 64-65

Page 76-77

placed within or around traditional containers such as baskets, unique trays, and elegant serving pieces. These are abundant and easily obtainable for collectors to acquire. Some may be cherished family heirlooms. Others are discards found at thrift shops. Many home decor shops and craft stores offer interesting "objects d'art" which can effectively be combined with village pieces. *Keep your eyes open to find the perfect accent!*

Even if the entire village can no longer be set up, most collectors retain their favorite building(s). Analyze them. They will have a theme that can be expanded. On your journeys through grandma's attic, adventures to early morning garage sales or fun excursions to second-hand stores, keep a list of your prized village pieces handy. When you see something that might compliment your piece(s), consider including it into a village collage. Particularly if the item is older, or gently used, it may have to be rejuvenated: weathered to make it look old or older as in a Halloween setting, or painted to make it look revitalized and fresh to fit into a new environment. *Be open to new ideas!*

Almost everyone has some flat space somewhere: bookcases, table tops, areas above china cabinets or on architectural features within the home. For the most part, the vignettes in this book are featured in room settings, providing a glimpse into how they fit into their surroundings. Most are extremely simple to create, not only conserving space, but also time once the building selection and accent pieces have been determined. As the classic saying goes, *"a picture is worth 10,000 words"*. Many of these vignettes are self explanatory. If you do not have the piece shown, substitute another. These are just a starting point to give wonderful ideas to assist in your new quests to be able to appreciate your pieces in a much different way.

Page 120-121

Page 86

Page 142-145

Chapter 1:
- Village Pieces -
Plus Related Items Equal Interesting Vignettes

display/photos by John Michael Sanders

*An antique sleigh is the central focal point of this Alpine display.
The sleigh rests on a custom-made box. Village pieces surround*

*L*ooking through family attics, antique stores and thrift stores, it would not be surprising to find items that could enhance one or several village pieces. On the next several pages, there are numerous interesting couplings, commencing with old fashioned sleighs and sleds - the perfect accents for a winter village setting. There are several - in different sizes and styles, which would work well as floor and/or table displays.

*them. Pieces of styrofoam were used to fill the interior of the
sleigh - forming levels to set the buildings and tobaggon sled.*

John Michael Sanders, created the sleigh display featured
above and on the previous pages. A fairly large sleigh, he placed
several Alpine Village pieces within it, then expanded the village
on three sides by adding chunks of styrofoam to surround it. More
buildings and numerous trees were placed at various angles to
make a very interesting and inviting vignette. The result is a beautiful display taking less time than a typical village set up.

The easy part is putting the buildings into the sleigh after it was filled with styrofoam to build up the elevations and the electrical cording was hidden. The hard part is finding a dynamic sleigh like the one pictured above. It is awesome!

This gorgeous sleigh features pieces from the North Pole Woods collection. The display was created by Richard Puckett, Jr. Scrap pieces of styrofoam can be used to fill the interior, but once the height has been achieved so the buildings can be viewed properly, the styrofoam must be cut exactly to the opening. If the display is placed next to a wall, the electrical cording can be secured on the backside of the sleigh.

The larger trees toward the back provide a backdrop for the buildings. Cords can be hidden by evergreen picks, as well. Battery lighting is best, especially if the vignette is to be viewed from all four sides which would be the case with centerpieces and many table displays.

display/photos by Richard Puckett, Jr.

Dear Santa,
All I want for Christmas
is world Peace.......but if you
want to leave me anything,
please leave things for my
Christmas village
Val

***Looks like Santa filled this sleigh with some very nice additions
to the McFadden village collection!*** *display/photo by Valerie McFadden*

Prior to Christmas 2012, Valerie McFadden found this sleigh on one of her shopping adventures. It inspired her to create a vignette around it, but what could be placed into it? After some consideration, she decided on the theme. She would ask Santa to fill it with something for her village. It appears Santa complied. After all, she left him a glass of milk and a variety of cookies. Looks like he enjoyed them, too! How could he resist? Two little green boxes and a green pine tree fit nicely into her sleigh.

Although this sleigh is quite small, there is still room for Santa's Sleigh Maker piece and accessories. *display/photo by Sue Chretien*

This wooden sleigh display created by Sue Chretien is just large enough for one building and a couple of related accessories. Dress it up with some pine boughs, ornaments, ribbon and other festive adornments, and the Christmas Holiday centerpiece or table decoration is complete. The building sets on a styrofoam round encircled with a coordinated ribbon. White candles provide a striking contrast to the red and green of the vignette and add a vertical component to the numerous curves and horizontal lines of the sleigh.

display/photo by Susie Clough O'Brien

- A Coffee Table Glass Resting on Top of a Flexible Flyer Sled Forms the Base of this Wonderful Display -

Susie Clough O'Brien's display is placed in front of the family fireplace. It features the three cornerstone pieces of the North Pole Village along with several accessory pieces. The actual base is a Flexible Flyer - a 1976 Christmas present for her daughter. It is 48" long with a piece of oval beveled coffee table glass measuring 44" x 32" which is set on top of the classic sled, angled in front of the fireplace. *Santa's Workshop* is on top of a piece of oval styrofoam 13' x 10" x 4". The white bricks forming the face of the fireplace frame the display, while the large white snowflakes toward the front bring the display forward. The white design elements balance and unite the vignette. The green ceramic Christmas tree in the background belonged to Sue's Mother-In-Law. It is placed on top of a Milk Glass compote from the 1960s.

Susie supplied a bit of history on the sled. Samuel Leeds Allen patented the Flexible Flyer in 1889. Allen began producing sleds in his farm equipment factory to keep his workers busy during the winter months. He developed many prototypes before he created the flexible flyer. The sleds did not sell well until he began marketing them to the toy departments of department stores. In 1915, around 120,000 Flexible Flyers were sold, and almost 2,000 were sold in one day.

In 1968, Leisure Group of Los Angeles, California bought the S. L. Allen Company. Leisure Group continued to produce the sleds in Medina, Ohio. In 1973, a group of private investors bought Leisure Group's toy division and started manufacturing the sleds under the name "Blazon Flexible Flyer" in West Point, Mississippi. Susie's sled probably dates within this time period. In 1993, Roadmaster purchased the production rights and moved the manufacturing plant to Olney, Illinois. In 1998, production was moved to China. As of 2012, Flexible Flyers are still made in China and sold by Paricon, Inc in South Paris, Maine - for village collectors, too!

The locomotive display was based on a cherished Lionel train John Michael received as a Christmas gift. It incorporates two Department 56 train stations. display/photo by John Michael Sanders

- Containers to Accent a Stylistic Vignette Come in all Shapes and Sizes -

This Lionel Train display was an homage to John Michael Sander's father, as well as, his own love of model trains. For Christmas, 1954, Mike received a Lionel train. His dad passed away shortly thereafter, when John Michael was very young. It remained a cherished set, however, the train was lost in a house fire. As time passed, the search was on to replace that vintage locomotive and the cars it towed.

"I took a photo of the engine to train stores in the St Louis area and was able to find an exact match. After D56 came out with the Snow Village Lionel Electric Train Store, I got the idea to build the display, combining all the elements."

John Michael constructed the locomotive display in his workshop. It was modeled after the front end of the actual Lionel train locomotive that encircles the base on the 27" diameter track. He made a drawing to take measurments. Power tools used were a radial arm saw, jig saw, belt sander and drill.

The cavity in the back was an unexpected addition. After he cut the circular shaped rear of the tank, he also cut the "O" shape on the back so he could gain access into the interior of the tank for the electrical wiring. It created the perfect location for a vignette featuring the Christmas in the City *Grand Central Railway Station*.

The entire display was constructed primarily of wood, including pine boards, birch plywood, and birch benderboard (very thin plywood that can be easily shaped into curved shapes) and laminate backerboard (essentially the base material used to make Formica® counter tops.)

It also contains metal parts: wire and metal rods, actual nuts and bolts, butterfly anchors, L brackets, tin cans and miscellaneous hardware. It also incorporates PVC pipe fittings. The snow is white shaved craft store styrofoam.

The base is 32" square and the constructed engine is 27" tall. The train encircling the display is O-27 scale. The unit rotates only about 180 degees, as John Michael did not want to make an electrical pass-through. The unit sits on a O shaped turntable, with power cord put through the open middle of it. It is kept close enough to the wall so it can only turn 180 degrees. Thus, the power cord does not get twisted. All the transformers for train and lights are in the base of the train. There is no light behind the Lionel store, however, there is a C-7 light behind the Grand Central Railway Station to halo light the interior of the tank which shines through the front.

The display rotates 180 degrees to allow the viewer to see a second display built into the interior of the locomotive. This vignette features the Grand Central Railway Station. John Michael painted the sky behind it and back lit it with a C-7 bulb which illuminates the front. Passengers are brought to the station by horse drawn sleighs. The snow is created by rubbing hard craft store styrofoam pieces together.

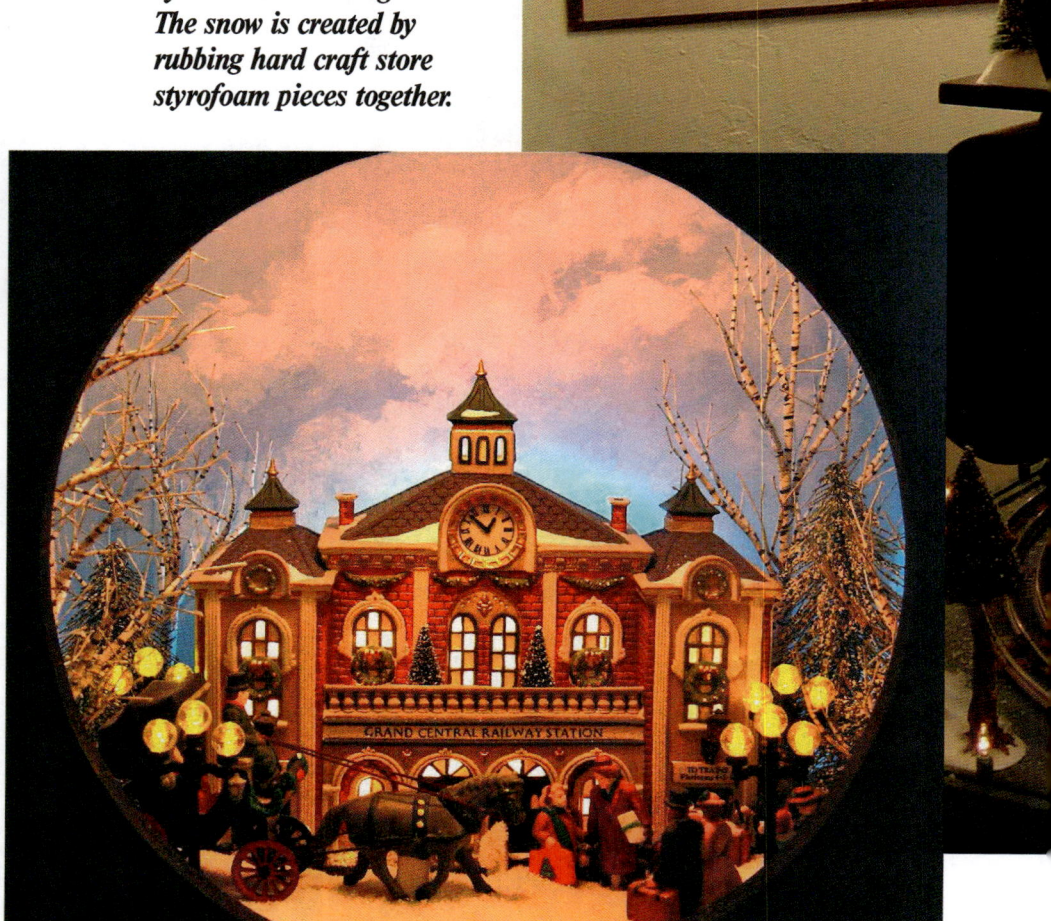

A Lionel 0-27 train encircles the entire display.

display/photos by John Michael Sanders

- Wooden Containers and Boxes Abound. Use Them as the Centerpiece of an Interesting Vignette -

Throughout the years, carpenters, cabinet makers and woodworkers would make wooden boxes for a multitude of uses in a variety of sizes. Some boxes, such as those made for holding silverware, jewelry or other precious items, were constructed of high quality woods, multiple inlaid wood pieces, or with burl insets. Many artistic woodworkers made toys like rocking horses, trains and trucks for family members from fine woods. Other wooden boxes were made from one of the more abundantly available woods. Some of these boxes and finely crafted toys have made their way into second-hand shops for others to enjoy. They all could be repurposed into a unique container for a village setting.

The painter's box located on the next page is one example of an imaginative vignette. It intermingles tubes of oil paints and artist's brushes with village accessory figures to develop a charming country scene. The talented Monique Pol of the Netherlands painted the background picture to fit the top lid of the painter's box. Compartments in the bottom were covered with a base of styrofoam which - in turn - was covered in landscaping materials from a model railroad store. Little painters gathered near the river's edge to record the tranquil scene for posterity. A photographer also captures the peaceful setting to film!

Colors from the landscaping materials and the trees - silk flowers from a craft store - used in the foreground were repeated in the background painting uniting the two sections of the vignette. Although not exactly the same tones, the pathway hues found in the foreground blends nicely with the reddish brown color of the box. The composition is dynamic, tying all the elements together!

This vignette, along with several other realistic vignettes created by Monique, also appears in the *Realistic Village Vignettes* book. This vignette not only uses an intriguing container as the centerpiece of the display, the realism is striking!

display/photos by Monique Pol

- Old Steamer Trunks Make Excellent Containers for Building a Village Vignette -

Valerie McFadden's daughter is a travel agent. Having an old steamer trunk was the perfect container for developing a display featuring a travel or resort setting. The smaller suitcase showcases the CIC *Paradise Travel Company* and a couple planning their honeymoon, while the larger trunk offers a glimpse of paradise. This is where one can find Santa after his grueling night of delivering toys for good little boys and girls, and to get out of the frigid North Pole!

Large steamer trunks may not be too accessible unless one is found in great grandma's attic, but a thrift store should have plenty of the mid 20th Century variety - hard cases with no wheels. Many buildings could work within a trunk. Choose a theme and get creative!

display/photos by Valerie McFadden

*- A Violin Case,
Some Sheet Music,
a Musical Themed Building
& an Orchestra -*

The violin in its case was found in a second hand store in the Netherlands. Mark de Vries filled the bottom section of the case with styrofoam, then added the *Swift's Stringed Instruments* building from Dickens' Village, along with various accessories. It makes a charming musical themed vignette. A sheet of music completes the setting to form a background. Put some of Vivaldi's Violin Concertos on the iPod to provide even more atmosphere. Speakers can go behind the case. Other string instrument cases could be substituted, or incorporate several instruments together.

- Just Add Vivaldi!

display/photos by Mark de Vries

Larger craft stores carry many items that work well with village pieces. This floor standing bird cage style comes in two sizes, opens from the top to allow fairly tall buildings and easy access to place coordinating pieces and some landscaping. There are also several other styles which are not as ornate.

display/photos by
Leigh Gieringer

- *Bird Cages: Dynamic Containers!* -

Some bird cages are huge and are actually meant for pet birds. But, if you have the space, numerous buildings could be set up within these large cages. Others are more decorative - with varying degrees of embellishments. They are accent pieces found in furniture stores, home decor stores, thrift and second hand stores, garden nurseries, as well as some larger craft stores and garage sales. Since these featured birdcages sit on the floor, they have a strong and striking vertical presence. They can be quite dramatic as a prop for displaying village pieces. Use both sizes together!

These cages open at the top to allow for the development of a simple scene. Tall buildings with a small footprint are perfect to enhance the display. This hotel piece fits perfectly, while a couple of shorter favorite Christmas in the City pieces could also be placed within the larger cage.

Another choice would be the pieces with the wrought iron motif in their design like the *Jambalaya Café* or *The 21 Club*. Dress it up with appropriate accessories. *The Bird Sellers* are featured in this one. Decorative feathered birds can be connected to the cage, coordinating with some appropriate ribbon or garland, if desired. *The Lilycott Garden Conservatory* is in the smaller cage on the previous page.

Surrounding the cages can be other items. Living plants could be set nearby. In front of the cages lower unique tables, such as a set of nesting tables, or some decorative boxes holding additional pieces could develop into a striking display. Or, merely stack styrofoam pieces at different elevations near the base similar to that which was placed around the sleigh on pages 3-5, to create an entire small village around it or them. A cloth or blanket of snow can camouflage the foam stacks and unify the vignette.

In a home decor store there are also metal lanterns with varying shapes, sizes and finishes to coordinate with one's choice of village piece(s) or accessories scene. Choose one to fit inside the container. More complimentary pieces can be placed around the lantern to expand the vignette.

Lanterns can also be found in many shapes and sizes, and even in different hues. Some are actually intended to contain an electrical bulb or candles, but they are a perfect container for placement of a village piece and related items since most already possess character in their designs and attractive coloring. Dress them up with silk flowers or garlands coordinating with the tones featured in the vignette. display/photo by Bob Eustice

- Lanterns also Make Interesting Packaging for Small Vignettes. A Wide Variety is Available! -

- A Cabin in the Woods -

Bob Eustice acquired a rustic lantern from a local nursery during the holiday period. It became the focal point of this vignette. The interior featured the New England Village *Mountain View Cabin* with *Display Anywhere Lighting* and the LeMax® figurine *Bringing Christmas Cheer*. Additional accessories included the deer from the *Woodland Wildlife Animals*; and a miniature squirrel, cardinal and dog. The *Limestone Lamps* were also included.

Winter Birch Trees and *Winter Lodge Pines* were incorporated and Woodland Scenics® Coarse Foam Turf (Light Green) was used for the ground cover. As a finishing touch, a woodland garland with evergreen leaves punctuated with small pine cones and red/white berry clusters was draped over the lantern.

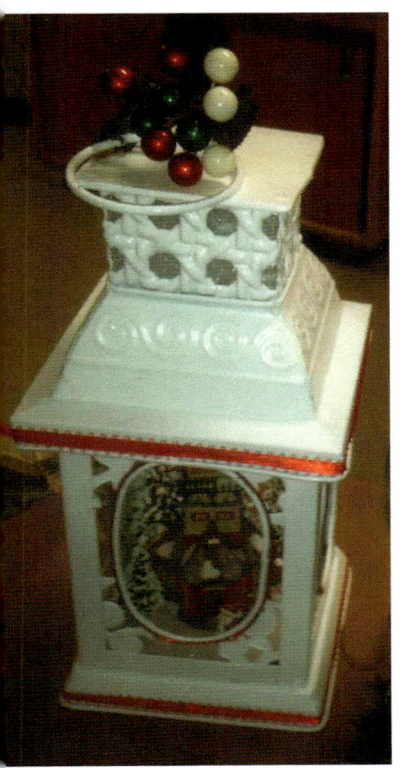

- Change the Appearance to Coordinate with the Theme -

Linda Roberts, saw potential in this lantern she located at a craft store. It began its life colored black, but she wanted to put a North Pole ornament into it. Thus, Linda painted it white, added a Christmas pick to the handle and some small red ribbon for contrast and to bring out the coloration of the mini *Santa's Lookout Tower*.

Since lanterns come in so many styles and colors, there is probably one to match most decors and buildings to be inserted. They have a small footprint, so can be placed almost anywhere. Detail them to correspond to the season or theme. Change them for variety!

display/photo by Linda Roberts

display/photo by Sue Chretien

A music theme is carried through on Sue Chretien's grand piano. Beethoven and the Peanuts characters band is quite a combination. Add a small Christmas Tree, some decorative Christmas

Chapter 2:
- It All Started
*   With Christmas -*
Holiday Vignettes

boxes, large peppermint trees and small porcelain trees to several North Pole buildings. It makes a wonderful display. Of course, kids of all ages just love several Snoopy Dogs surrounding the setting.

- Numerous North Pole Buildings
Lend Themselves as Focal Points
in a Stylistic Vignette . . . -

Most North Pole buildings are themed. Some feature candy, cookies, or other food based buildings making for happy tummy's to celebrate special Christmas festivities. These make wonderful kitchen accents. Several ideas can be found in Chapter 7 beginning on page 92. But, Santa typically brings good little boys and girls favorites from a range of toys like Bears and Dolls, Crayola®s, Play Doh®, LEGO®s, Barbie®, trains and other toy related buildings. North Pole factories and stores abound. Use these buildings accented by objects portraying the same theme such as the vignette featuring the *Teddy Bear Training Center* below. These small vignettes can fit into small areas and take mere moments to assemble. Several other toy related vignettes can be created and spread around the home, using the toy theme throughout. Toy store vignettes are also fun to develop. Tiny boats, trains, bears, dolls and other miniature items can be located throughout the year and

A Teddy Bear themed hat box can be found at craft stores during the Holiday season. Put the Teddy Bear Training Center on it, surrounded by several favorite Teddy Bears. A Teddy Bear themed tray forms the backdrop.
display/photos by
Frank Mapes

Create a Vignette Under a Christmas Tree

Table top Christmas Trees can be dressed up with your favorite building or buildings and accessories. The "snow" is packing material to protect a larger item during shipping.

display/photos by Leigh Gieringer

RIGHT: *Some children's books can fit right into a North Pole setting. This is the center "building" above. Perfect scale and coloration to blend right in.*

added around the building(s). An abundant selection of inexpensive minis are available during the Holidays or in dollhouse sections of a craft store. Or, look through the ornament section for ideas. Hallmark® has often offered tiny well-made trains to accent a toy store or *Toot's Model Train Manufacturing* building.

During the Christmas Holidays, seasonal books are also available. Some are die-cut like the one above. The size is perfect to add to a North Pole display. The strong color also blends, without the depth. From a distance, it looks just like another building - one unique to your village!

- *Monochromatic Displays*
Can Be Very Dramatic -

The Winters Frost Collection has a very unique appearance especially compared to other villages. It is as if the Gods of Winter blessed the entire village with its touch of dazzling white crystals. To date, there are no accessories developed exclusively to accompany these pieces. Some collectors populate this village with Snow Village inhabitants. However, most of those are shiny and brightly colored. They don't really fit well. Thus, it is the perfect village to incorporate into stylistic vignettes.

Start with a white tree. The one pictured is about 48" tall. It was decorated in all silver: several types of silver ornaments, silver picks, silver bows, and silver ribbons. It sits on a silver tree skirt with decorative silver gift boxes. Silver poinsettias and other silver accents complete the setting. Although the colors are quite similar, the textures provide contrast as light reflects off the different surfaces. There are a couple of strings of white lights on the tree, but are mostly hidden by the numerous attached items.

At the base of the tree sits the *Winters Frost Lighthouse* borrowed from Sharon Palenkas. It sets on two silver topped sparkled gift boxes. More pieces could be placed around the base of the tree if the tree would have 360° visibility. Gift boxes with different dimensions can be used to raise the buildings to different levels, or use pieces of styrofoam covered in silver fabric or wrapped in silver Holiday gift paper to obtain a variance in height. Snow covered trees of varying heights, and similar to the ones connected to the buildings, can be placed between them.

The inset picture on the next page shows a Snow Village church which is also effective because the palette is mostly white with a deep gray roof. The coloration compliments the setting! A selection of other pieces could also be used, such as the North Pole's *Real Artifical Tree Factory*. It's pastel tones, as well as its theme, are a perfect substitute!

displays/photos by
Leigh Gieringer

ABOVE: The frosty
coloration of the Winter's
Frost Winters Light
Lighthouse is the ideal
addition to a silver mono-
chromatic setting.
As an alternative, add
other silver elements like
the Santa on the right.
There are numerous silver
items available during
the Holidays! Use several!

- *Create Your Own Stylized Christmas Tree* -

Add several shelves to a triangular shape representing a stylized Christmas Tree. Paint the unit as below, or white for a flocked tree look. In this case, channels were added on the lower shelf to hold strings of mini lights. To expand it, two identical additional shelving units were added, one on each side for the overflow of buildings. *display/photos by John Michael Sanders*

Wooden shelves were made to showcase the North Pole Woods in the form of a stylistic Christmas Tree. When the tree shelves were filled, additional shelves were built to accommodate the overflow. This wall unit was built by John Michael Sanders. The shelves also contain his signature green coloration and inset mini-light.

display/photo by Debbie Shelgren

- *A Table Sized Christmas Tree Can be Enhanced with Village Pieces, and Coordinating Accessories* -

Numerous village pieces, or a planned village, can be placed under a large Christmas Tree, but many collectors no longer have room for a full sized tree. A small table top tree, or several small trees, can be placed in rooms throughout the house, or in entryways as a substitute or as the main attraction in smaller homes. At the base of a tree, place a single piece similar to the one Debbie Shelgren used on the previous page. The associated accessories make a pleasing, yet easy to create vignette. Or, multiple buildings can be placed near a small tree if the surface can accommodate them like a fireplace hearth or a larger entry case piece or bureau. Other Christmas related items can be incorporated into the setting.

If space allows, several small trees can effectively be grouped or placed in adjoining rooms. Buildings from the same village - especially those from the same series within the village can be featured. The trees will visually tie the buildings together. The trees can have at least one similar item, colors, ribbons, or ornaments to unify them. For instance, a red bow can top all trees. A matching red ribbon, blending with the bow can be strung throughout all trees. Red ornaments - or coordinating color - in varying shapes, finishes, etc., can be used to decorate each tree. The trees looked planned and are united. Vary the number of buildings under the trees. One larger building similar to the one in the photo can be put under one tree, while two tall buildings with a smaller foot prints can adorn another. Three buildings could fit under a third. All coordinate! Try them at different elevations in the groupings!

Another popular - and getting more so - are Santa Claus figures. Combine them with trees and village pieces. There is a numerous selection available in a variety of colors and dress to accent a setting. The Santas are considerable larger, but that only adds to the composition. Coordinate the colors of Santa's outfit with the colors of the piece or pieces in the vignette. There are several samples on the following pages.

- Santa Claus Figures
are a Large Part of Christmas.
Combine them with Village Pieces. -

The Santa in this vignette is completely scratch built by John Michael Sander's sister. The head, mittens and boots are all hand painted porcelain - right down to his eyelashes. His attire is also hand made. This Santa figure makes a wonderful addition to several North Pole buildings - all toy building pieces: *Toots Model Train Mfg.*, *Jack in the Box, Plant #2,* and *Checking it Twice Wind-up Toys*. The coordinating accessories, as well as other miniature toys, compliment the setting. On the tree are small ornaments continuing the toy theme. All sit on an area the size of an end table.

The train that goes around Santa's feet carries the Hallmark® brand. Besides the already animated D56 pieces, the Hallmark train, the two elves on the round toboggan and the balloon are also animated. John Michael used two separate motors to propel these pieces. The two metal antique reproduction toys were part of a set that Department 56® made.

Additional animation was added for an awesome vignette.

The head, mittens and boots - made of porcelain - are all hand painted. Merge the Santa Claus figure with toy related buildings from the North Pole, add small toys that illustrate the building's theme and some antique toy heirlooms or finds. display/photos by John Michael Sanders

Thick cut slabs of mesquite wood - approximately 12" in diameter - form the bases of these intriguing western influenced table decorations. Thus, they can fit almost anywhere. Each one is unique. Items are secured onto the base so they will not move.

The slabs of wood are large enough to put the Santa adorned authentic leather cowboy boot, a full sized building with an accessory and some trees. Or, several miniature ornaments can be substituted. Dawn often finds appropriate plaques to enhance her vignettes.

- Add a Western Influence -

A part of the old west tradition is carried through Dawn Savage's intriguing table displays. She looks for authentic leather cowboy boots at thrift stores and repurposes them into these stunning vignettes which fit perfectly on a corner table. She couples a boot with a Santa Claus, Father Christmas, Kris Kringle or any number of special Santas from other lands. They are all handsomely dressed! He is mounted in the boot. Most of Dawn's displays are created using a village piece with at least one coordinating accessory. The choice of building coordinates with the chosen Santa's outfit. Others feature several miniature ornaments. Snow Babies are also very popular in her displays. Each display is unique, and stands about three feet tall. Three of them are pictured here.

Thick slabs of mesquite wood - with the bark still connected - form the heavy base of most of them since mesquite is more readily available in Tucson, Arizona where she lives. She has also used birch or aspen for the bases, however, they are much harder to locate in southern Arizona.

Several of them also feature Christmas messages, color coordinated to the building(s) used. They can easily be placed in a box for storage during the off season. Or, appreciate them year around!

displays by Dawn Savage

This vignette used basically the same items as the cover image, however the white tree was replaced with a green one and it is decorated differently, showing versatility in elements used and altering placement. display/photos by Leigh Gieringer

- Santas Come in Many Colors -

The red and green of Christmas has been expanded to numerous other color selections. Colors can match or blend with just about every decor. A peacock theme has become omnipresent recently. Real peacock feathers are attached to ornaments and picks: the blue and yellow-green colors are artfully used to compliment the theme. Stylistic versions have been incorporated into angels, metallic birds, candle holders and more. The Peacock Santa is stunning - dressed in the theme colors and accented with real feathers. He is a great addition to the peacock theme.

However, the North Pole buildings that blend with this color combination are very limited. The *Real Artifical Tree Factory* comes closest with its yellow-green trim. The walls of the building are a light tint of gray, which blends with Santa's beard. These two elements attract attention, making them the focal points of the display. The other surrounding elements unite and compliment them.

This is the cover version for an easy comparison to the photo on page 40. The biggest difference is the use of a white tree in the cover image, while the one to the left has a green tree. Both work, but many viewers will gravitate to one or the other. Many items are currently available with a Peacock motif.

Most of the North Pole buildings are designed with Christmas red and green roofs and trim. Most of the Santa figures are also dressed in tones of red, green, golds or off white. Thus, there are numerous options to creating a North Pole/Santa Claus vignette. Find a Santa - or several - you like and coordinate with favorite North Pole buildings and their accessories, and add other related items.

display/photos
by Debbie Shelgren

Which came first:
the village collection
or the Santa collec-
tion? This SV jewelry
store does have the
place of honor on a
glass compote. Is
this a hint for Santa
to bring diamonds
and rubies?

North Pole may have a natural coupling to a Santa/Village vignette, but other buildings can also be featured with St. Nick.

Debbie Shelgren has numerous Santa figures. She showcases her collection in and on a book case with Snow Village's *Pearlson's Jewelry* as the central attraction. Placed on a circular piece of styrofoam, it rests on a vintage glass footed dish. The building is accented with numerous pieces of costume jewelry and adorned with Holiday garland, accompanied by several Santas dressed in "ruby" red - trimmed in "diamond" white.

There are jewelry stores in many villages that can be substituted next to Santa. After all, jewelry is often associated with Christmas gift giving. A building such as the Dickens' Village *J.D. Nichols Toy Shop* - or a toy store from another village - would have tremendous potential to be associated with Santa. Try the Victorian Christmas Series buildings, as well!

- Pair Village Pieces with Nutcrackers or Dolls -

Santas are not the only Christmas related figures that can be merged with village pieces. Nutcrackers also come in a variety of shapes, colors and sizes. Several village buildings feature them!

Wood carved Nutcrackers have been around since at least the 15th century. The original Nutcrackers were derived from rural forested areas of Germany and were portrayed as strong figures representing soldiers, knights or kings - the guardians of the people. They could possibly already be a part of many households as they were passed down through the generations. Colorful new ones abound during the Holidays, so they are also easy to find.

The Alpine's *Nikolausfiguren* - (Nicholaus Figurines) or *Nussknacker Werkstatt* (the Nutcracker Factory) are ideal companions for a variety of Nutcrackers. The North Pole *Nutcracker Factory* is a logical compliment to this theme. Look for items with the same or accenting coloration. Around the Holidays, many items can be found with the Nutcracker theme - holiday boxes and bags, and more to add to the setting.

display/photo by Leigh Gieringer

Dominant red and green tones of the North Pole make it easy to add other items containing hues of those same tones. Nutcrackers are a favorite, especially with the Nutcracker Factory (featured left) or the Brite Lights Bulb Factory with its strong red and green tones. Colorful boxes provide platforms to place buildings, or just accent the color palette. display/photo by Leigh Gieringer

Dolls have always been a favorite collectible. Many village collectors have inherited porcelain dolls, retained their childhood favorites or collect the newer designer dolls. There are also numerous doll or toy related village pieces. Combine them! Victoria's Doll House (CIC) and its accessory piece is featured here. It is surrounded by Virginia Martin's doll collection that once belonged to her mother.

display/photos by Virginia Martin

An antique rocking chair becomes the base for Marie's Doll Museum - from the North Pole Village. Add a couple of family heirloom dolls. The result is a very simple, but effective vignette. It could be expanded by adding the Elfin Toy Museum, Barbie's Boutique or other doll related buildings placed on colorful boxes artistically placed. display/photo by Frank Mapes

There are many types of dolls available to accent any doll related piece. Besides the dolls of one's childhood, or heirloom collectibles passed down through the generations, modern reproductions can also become part of an exciting and meaningful vignette. Adding favorite dolls - or other toys to their themed piece(s) - might also be a way to get the younger generations interested in village displaying and appreciation. Putting the pieces together is easy, but the memories last forever!

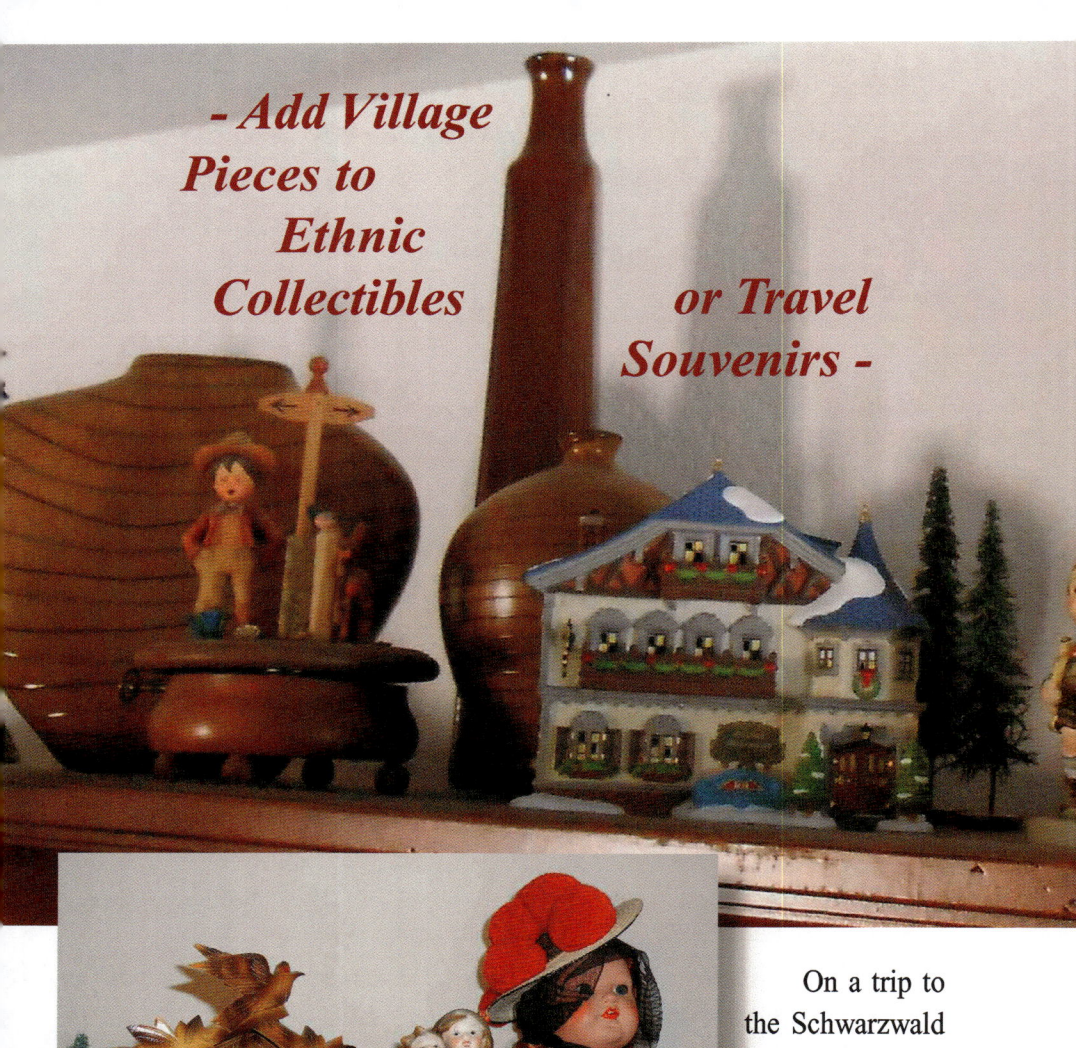

- Add Village Pieces to Ethnic Collectibles

or Travel Souvenirs -

Other regional items can be incorporated into the setting such as the Black Forest Cuckoo Clock. Look for items from your heritage and group them with a themed piece.

On a trip to the Schwarzwald (Black Forest) in Germany, one might stay at the Alpine Village's *Gasthof Mittenwald*. The hotel is placed on top of a bookcase, surrounded by a traditional Black Forest doll - circa early 1960s - wear-

Expand the setting by adding the Black Forest Tower and other related accessories.

display/photos by Leigh Gieringer

ing a Bollenhut*, a few heirloom Hummel Figurines, a Black Forest Music Box playing the *Happy Wanderer*, and some background pottery - not old / not German, but the color accents the building tones. And, they provides some height and texture!

*NOTE: The dress consists of a dirndl skirt with a floral design, fitted bodice or vest, blouse, apron, and a Bollenhut (wide-brimmed hat decorated with woollen balls or pom-poms). Red pom-poms are worn by unmarried women and black by married ones.

An artist's paper mock up is placed next to the real piece to form this striking vignette. Both sides are almost identical, except the

Chapter 3:
- Place in Curio Cabinets -
Glass Boxes, Shelves & Table Tops

*T*here are numerous places throughout the house that can hold a vignette. The most obvious are cabinets, shelves and table tops.

left side was recreated in black and white. The glass box protects the display. *display/photo by Ellen Somerwill and Linda Roberts*

- Two Heads Can Be Better Than One -

Ellen Somerwill, a member of Queen City Villagers, Ohio, always wanted one of the artist's paper mock-ups. She was fortunate enough to be the winning bidder on one in a Ronald McDonald House fund raiser. After she acquired it, she wondered what she was going to do with it?

"I wanted the piece to be displayed versus packed up like so many of my other houses. I didn't want it to get dirty or exposed to the elements. I had this box that I had bought at a Thrift Store. Perhaps that would work for a display."

Linda Roberts, another club member, looked at the paper mock-up and the finished piece and said *"black and white"*. It took off from there. We divided the box in half doing one side black and white, and the other side in color. Everything was to be identical on both sides with the exception of the color.

Duplicate accessories had to be purchased. Imagine painting the accessories black and white. Adding and painting leaves on trees to have a green one and a black one.

The paper mock-up did not have the water sections. The ladies had to make them using EnviroTex Lite®. What should be used for the sides of the water to make it look like the finished piece? Caulking. They needed to find little stones and place them in the same positions as on the finished piece in the caulk. Painting blue around each stone as in the finished piece.

Mirrors were glued to the back to make it appear larger and reflect the back of the pieces. There's actually a dividing line in the mirrors.

In the end, it didn't stay identical. The bird on the black and white side stayed red. The old saying *"Two heads are better than One"* really helped pull off this display.

- *Construct a Wood Framed Shadow Box* -

Change the theme. Change the background. Change the Building!

Locate a frame which matches the room decor. Craft and frame stores have an abundant collection from which to choose. Sides can be durable wood or made from styrofoam. See page 150 to see how Joe Meyers changed this box. display/photo by Joe Meyers

Any flat surface can be brought to life with a building, trees and an accessory or two. Place several small chests, old stereo speakers, or decorative tables of varying height together. It is more interesting if they are placed at different angles. Add candles, greenery, or silk flowers for color and texture. In this case, the desired effect was derived by using neutral colors picking up the soft cream colors prevalent in both churches. The light color contrasts nicely with the blackish tones of the case pieces. display/photo by Leigh Gieringer

- Cars, Trucks, Cycles, & Boats -
Popular Themes: Lots of Choices! -

A fireplace mantel is a dynamic location to build a small display with related buildings like the Snow Village farm scene above. It can easily be changed, updated or altered.

Anne Saxe has been building 1, 2 or 3 building vignettes for a very long time. The smaller ones were created so she could enjoy her collection while she was planning a much larger room sized village. She has several areas throughout her home suitable for vignettes, and has now decided that developing these vignettes is a much better alternative for her.

One location is over the fireplace. Fireplaces, by their very nature, attract attention even when there isn't a roaring fire in them, especially on a cold, winter's eve. What better place to add village pieces then to the mantel. It provides a space for several buildings in a themed display. It is simple to create and can be changed at will. The display above is slightly larger than her aver-

Styrofoam was added to the base under the Buck's County buildings allowing more versatility with cords and trees.

displays/photos by Anne Saxe

age vignette, but a lot smaller than a normal table - or room-sized display. It shows Anne's farm year-round display. It included the Snow Village *Dairyland*, the *Dairy Barn*, *Gothic Farmhouse*, and *Abners Farm Implements* along with a generous assortment of cows, rural vehicles, and more. The Buck's County buildings later were substituted and placed on styrofoam.

Top: On a vintage record cabinet, Anne Saxe made a scene using Shelley's Diner with numerous vehicles. Since it is non-seasonal, it can remain throughout the year. However, it is easy to move the vignette to a new location (Lower), and reposition or change the accessories. A new vignette can be set up in the old setting focusing on another favorite building or a new theme: a wonderful way to rotate pieces and keep vignettes fresh.

displays/photos by Anne Saxe

display/photos by Jerry Fernon

Many villages now feature Harley Davidson® buildings. Here is one way to dramatically showcase those buildings.

Jerry Fernon used an actual Harley Davidson® tire for the base of his display. The white material around the perimeter represents snowbanks resulting from a snowplow cleaning the parking lot. The lights were made from a nasal inhaler and wire nuts along with plastic tubing for the light poles.

display/photos by Carolyn and Dick Dooley

Besides the *Harley Davidson®* buildings, there are other car related buildings such as gas stations and car dealerships, as well as the use of cars in parking lots as was seen in the *Shelley's Diner* display, or traveling along a roadway. There are numerous village cars, but scaled vehicles are also available through many other sources, ranging from classics to the lastest models. Carolyn and Dick Dooley coupled the *CIC Hensly Cadillac & Buick Dealership* and the *Royal Oil Company* with a Fourth of July picnic.

ABOVE: *The wooden fence in the background frames the display. Flags and the blue and red picks provide atmosphere to the picnic area.*

LEFT: *Independence Hall, or one or more of the American Pride Collection buildings can be combined with Williamsburg figures as a patriotic or Fourth of July vignette. The paraders shown here are similar to, but are not D56.*

display/photo by Leigh Gieringer

The base level of this clever display was created with poker chips. Lighter blue chips were laid out to form the water upon which the boat is placed. A number of darker chips form the platforms for the other casinos. The green chips separate the two areas, but also serve as an attractive design element. The latter two areas were stacked to give dimension and develop a shoreline.

- *Welcome to Las Vegas!* -

Styrofoam, cut into a six-sided shape, forms the base of this display just large enough to place the four pieces comfortably.
display/photo by Jeff McCann

A display created by Jeff McCann uses the *High Roller Riverboat Casino* from Snow Village and several other casinos from the Christmas in the City village. Las Vegas is a favorite vacation spot, and what better way to remember the fun in Vegas than by incorporating the famous *Welcome to Las Vegas* sign and landmark into your village. Jeff used poker chips for the water and land, and card decks actually used in one of the real casinos for the perimeter of the base.

Chapter 4:
- *Books* -
Aren't Just for Reading!

Although this display does not feature any books, the wreath above it contains musical items, perhaps even some sheet music could be added. Can't you just imagine a choir singing "Away in the Manager" or "Little Town of Bethlehem"? The addition of non-village unrelated items can give the display an entirely different feel. display/photo by Sue Chretien

*B*ooks or stories can enhance a village theme such as the *Little Town of Bethlehem* vignettes on these two pages, or they can be incorporated into the setting. Charles Dickens has written numerous stories reflecting England in the mid to later 1800s. Department 56® has brought some realism to several of them. Village collectors bring them to life!

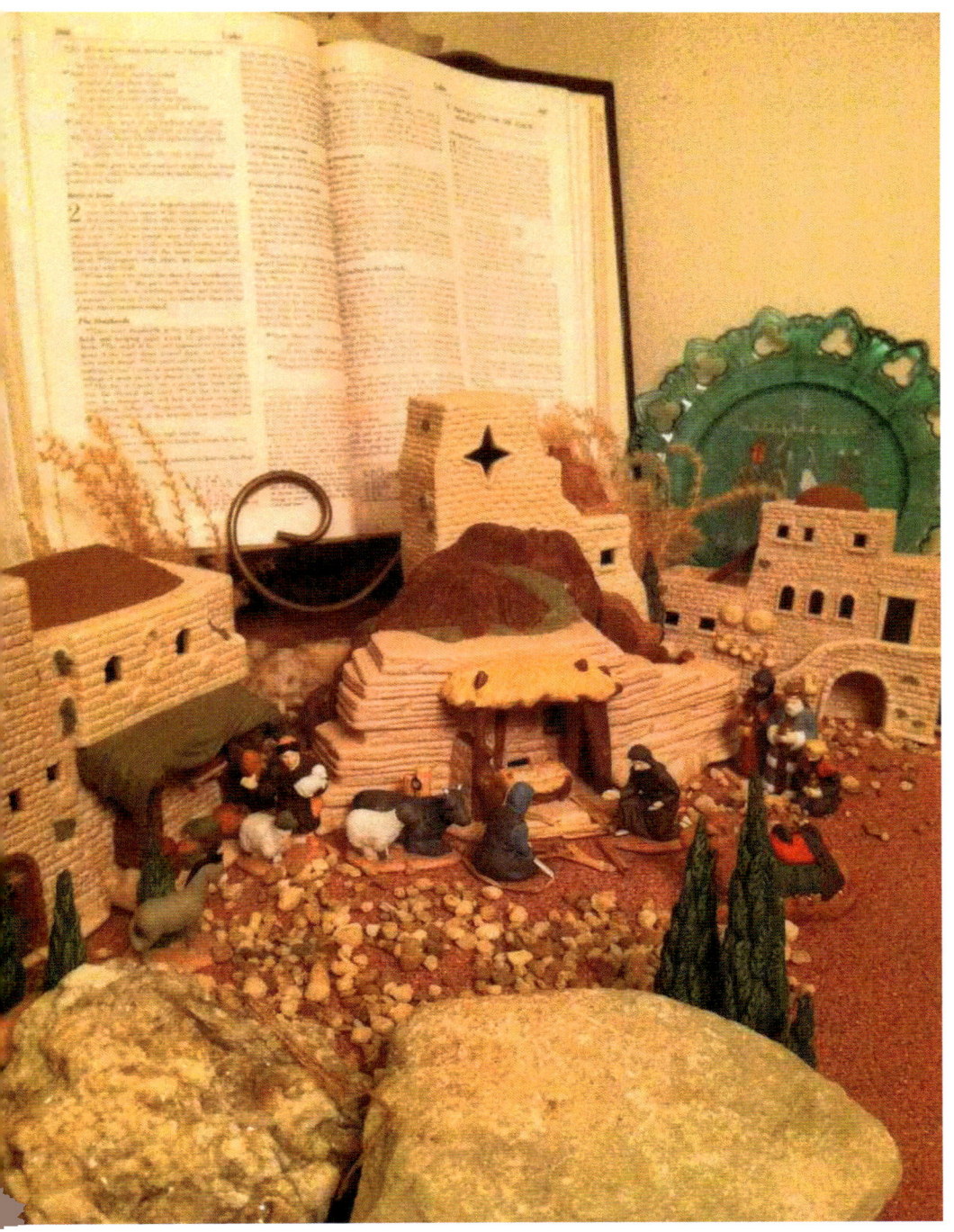

Sue O'Brien also displays the Original Little Town of Bethlehem buildings, but includes a copy of the Bible. It makes a striking additon and provides an authentic backdrop to the setting.

display/photo by Susie Clough O'Brien

- *Use Architectural Features for Vignettes!* -

Many homes have architectual features such as a built-in niche. However, they can be problematic for collectors of miniature villages. They are very tall and extremely narrow. There is not much room to build elevations to balance their disproportionate dimensions. The buildings would be dwarfed as they sat on the base of the niche. Ray Bukovszky solved that dilemma - in style!

The background was pre-painted prior to moving into the

home. Ray wanted to use the Christmas Carol buildings. He located a poster, found several Dickens books in new and used book stores, and collected several Buyer's Choice dolls having the Christmas Story theme. Placing the books on the base of the niche was the easy part. Drilling the two books being held up by the twisted cording was a bit more difficult. It required two pieces of quarter inch plywood: one on the top, the other on the bottom, to hold the covers and pages tightly as the 3/8" drill bit did its thing. The book store owner was horrified when told of his plan! The cording was strung through the books and secured. Hooks were placed in the top of the niche to hold the cords and hanging books. The tassles add color and a finishing touch. Buildings and other elements were placed.

A niche can become an ideal location to showcase a series of related items.

display/photos by Ray Bukovszky

The Christmas Story theme is enhanced by Dickens storybooks, characters, and a poster. Although an unusual proportion for a village setting, this space was developed into an exquisite vignette.

Virginia Martin incorporated copies of Dickens' The Christmas Story (top photo) and David Copperfield (lower photo) to the settings featuring buildings and accessories from these respective series. The Nickolas Nickleby duo and accessories were also showcased as they were set into a basket (top of the next page).

displays/photos by Virginia Martin

- Dickens & Other Stories -

display/photo by Virginia Martin

- The big, bad wolf won't blow this one down! -

*The Storybook
Village T.L. Pigs
Brick Factory was
themed from the
English Fairy Tales -
The Three Little
Pigs. Ellen created
a house of straw
and one of sticks to
accompany the
piece, as well as
developed a little
pig community and
included a copy of
the story.*

display/photo by Ellen Somerwill

Chapter 5:
- Containers -
Compliment
Village Pieces

*W*hich comes first: selecting a village piece or pieces, or finding an ideal container to accent them? Many times, the inspiration is derived from locating that perfect accent piece, but identifying a favorite village piece can provide insight into what type of container would make a dynamic pairing!

This exquisite vignette, created by Mark de Vries, was built into a relatively small wooden bookcase which was shaped like a boat. The shelves were removed and it was placed on its side instead of upright. Because of its realism, it is also featured in the Realistic Village Vignettes book, with step by step instructions on its construction. display/photo by Mark de Vries

The waterfront floor vignette features a couple New England buildings and a party tub painted blue. Several other water related items enhance the display.

display/photo by
Mary Jewell

Party tubs are an excellent choice to use to build a container display. This fantastic idea was created by Mary Jewell. The blue color gives a subtle indication of the ocean on a bright sunny day. Add some pylons wrapped with rope to hold them together. The posts are actually pool noodles that were spray painted brown. Mary placed pieces of styrofoam within the tub to build it up to a level that would favorably showcase the buildings. Real sand was placed near the buildings. Plastic plants from pet shops were used for the foliage behind the buildings. The stylized lobster, fish netting and sign were purchased at a craft store.

Lighthouses are popular subjects for vignettes. This one is a functioning lamp display and was also featured in the Realistic Village Vignettes book with instructions on how to create it. It makes a dymanic container vignette.

display/photos by Philip Renninger

- A Golfing Theme Accents a Study for a Golfer! -

The wall paper was accented with the Dickens' Village clubhouse.
display/photo by Barbara Westberg

The study in the home the Westbergs purchased years ago, included a chair rail. A golfing border was selected from a wallpaper book since golfing was chosen to be the theme of the room. When the Dickens' Village *Burwicken Clubhouse* came out, Barbara Westberg knew that was the perfect building to compliment the wallpaper border. The scene is placed on an antique refrigerator (an old fashioned icebox) originally purchased to be used to store drink supplies and serve drinks. A basket weave table runner serves as the base of the display since quite often the fairways in Texas are various shades of beige and/or brown.

Although the Dickens' Village *Burwickglen Clubhouse* is the focal point, several related accessories are also used: the three piece Dickens' Village *Par for the Course*, the *Putting Green* which includes a sand trap, a rake and a flag pole (to be numbered by the purchaser from 1 to 18). A United States flag and flag pole, as well as, the leafed tree from the *Spring/Summer Landscape Set*, and three pine trees from the *Pine Trees with Cones* set were also included. A golf lamp provides light and finishes the setting.

- *The Ultimate Container!* -

Many people do not use the master bath tub for its intended purpose, thus, the space may be available for creating a magnificent display. *display/photos by Jeff and Sue Chretien*

Sometimes one of the most overlooked containers is one we pass by each day – the bathtub! For the past couple of years, the Chretiens have done displays in their master tub. The base elements are the same. Jeff, cut two-by-fours that would cross the tub and give sturdy support for the two inch styrofoam that would be the base, and designed it so that if the tub were deep, Sue could work on the back half first, and then slide the trusses for the front half into place and complete the display. The first year, she did the crowded city of London, with a whopping 75 houses and accessories displayed. In the picture above, Sue wanted to use the Tower Bridge of London, and of course, it being in the bathtub, the logical thing was to use all of the water-front type buildings. The water was done using clear silicone caulking. Sue states, *"Every morning as I got ready for work and was putting on my makeup, I would gaze at my industrious waterfront of London, and I could almost hear the fish monger selling his freshly caught fish."*

NOTE: Since the electrical was dropped down into the tub, and then snaked out to the nearest outlet, be certain that the water could not actually run. The Chretiens turned off the water to the tub. If you can't turn off the water, make certain that your trusses safely ensconce the faucet so there is no danger of the water being accidently turned on while you're running the light cords.

- *A Lighthouse in a Container!* -

The inspiration for this display was a picture. The container was filled with canned insulation foam at an angle to the sides. It expands at least five times the initial application.

After an appropriate container was selected, a lighthouse was found to accent it. Insulation foam was sprayed into it. After the foam curred, the water was painted light blue. Depressed areas were colored dark blue. Some of the higher points were painted white for breaking waves. After the paint dried, the entire area was covered with Realistic Water®. Black rocks were added and small pieces of cotton glued in between. Once dried, the cotton was pulled up to give a break-ing wave effect. Final detailing was added.

*display/photos by
David and Jane Morton*

One of the focal points of this display is the funeral where the casket is being placed into a grave. *display/photos by Don Rush*

Although this display is not set into a basket or tub, it fits nicely on a bay window seat enclosure, another good spot to convert into a small village setting. This display combines several Dickens' Village pieces from Department 56® with LeMax® accessories, and is surrounded by custom mountains designed and

- Hand-Made Detail Accents a Vignette! -

This effect is a natural in a Halloween display. A blackened coffin can be partially open with skulls and bones scattered nearby!

constructed by Don Rush. He also made all the trees from air filters. The instructions are in the *Realistic Village Vignettes* book, along with some of his other awesome displays.

Don also made the cemetery and casket above, which is being lowered into a grave dug out of the styrofoam base.

When one thinks of doing a container display, the first types of container that comes to mind are baskets. There are so many available in all sizes and shapes - even a wide selection of colors. How do you select the perfect one? The examples in the next two chapters should shed some light on that question.

Chapter 6:
- Combine -
With
Baskets,
Trays &
More

The North Pole piece used in this basket display is *Mrs. Claus' Greenhouse*. Barbara Benjamin found the basket years ago at a shop in San Antonio, Texas. The basket is 16.5" to the top of the handle and 14" round. The opening is 14" side to side and 12" front to back. The size is large enough to fit a fairly large building, that is not too tall. Note how well the handle frames the building, bringing further attention to it. The green color makes it a perfect choice for a North Pole piece, but pieces from other villages with similar tones would also work well.

Barbara filled the basket with styrofoam to form a base for the greenhouse, about four or five layers cut to fit half of the basket. She put two 3" pots of artificial poinsettias in the back half of the basket, and placed the greenhouse on the styrofoam. The exposed foam was covered with moss. Sprigs of mistletoe and greens were placed around the greenhouse. Barbara inserted various picks of artificial greens, red apples, and pine cones around the base of the basket. The greenhouse elf sits on an upturned small basket placed nearby. She added an English tin by Silver Crane Designs. The *Delivering the Poinsettias Truck* heads toward the greenhouse. The vignette is displayed on the end of her kitchen island. It took approximately a half hour to create.

This large green basket creates a festive Holiday vignette.
display/photo by Barbara Benjamin

A beautifully embossed tin container, filled with floral foam, and then topped with white styrofoam, makes the perfect base for Melinda's Poinsettias and Mistletoe. Silk floral poinsettias were easy to poke into the styrofoam. Display Anywhere Lighting was used. It took about a half an hour to assemble.

display/photo by Sue Chretien

White, furry fabric serves as the base of this interesting vignette. It matches the trim of the Kringles Christmas Ornament Design Studio. Although it sets on a table, it could also be placed in a Christmas basket. Just add trees and a few other accessories.

display/photo by Debbie Shelgren

Roughened styrofoam bases could fit into shallow round baskets, but instead, these two Holiday centerpieces sit directly on a table. The top one is enhanced with extra greenery, brilliant red flowers and Holiday picks, to give it a striking and, dramatic effect. Change the appearance by substituting different buildings, accessories and/or their surroundings. Or, coordinate the centerpiece trim to the china and placemats. The lower vignette is merely adorned with festive trees for simplicity.

displays/photos by Debbie Shelgren

The Oriental influenced basket works well with Snow Village's Lucky Dragon Restaurant. The red in the orchids surrounding the basket, as well as, the red silky material under the display, plus the red within the lid accent the red trim in the building and the beautiful Geisha welcoming their guests. display/photo by John Michael Sanders

Add other themed items with an Oriental buildings for a very simple vignette. display/photo by Leigh Gieringer

TOP: This vignette uses a Longaberger basket for a New England scene. The brown tones of the buildings blend with the brown of the basket. INSET: The decorative ribbon picks up the colors in the cranberry bog. LOWER: The "Gone With The Wind" theme features the Tara Façade and pewter Civil War soldiers.

displays/photos by Terry and Nancy Hellman

Although this fabulous display, created by Monique Pol is also featured in the Realistic Village Vignettes book, it is included in the Stylistic Village Vignettes book because it is built in a wooden tray, which is then placed on a similarly colored plant basket. It is positioned on the floor like an end table in the room so it can be enjoyed. The old barnwood coloration is perfect for a Dickens' display because much of London is centuries old. Smoke, smog and weathering takes its toll. The container matches the feel of the display. display/photos by Monique Pol

A lot of detail can be placed in small areas!

It can easily be switched to another set of buildings with a different theme. The "how-to" techniques can be found in the other book.

This basket has an interesting shape - perfect to create a village scene in it. This one sits on the floor to light up an otherwise dark area. display/photo by Charles McFadden

The Potter's Tea Seller was placed on an antique tray. Linda Roberts used a small teapot that belonged to her Great-Grandmother. The D56 Display Anywhere Lighting provides the illumination. Since this display is portable, it can also be used as a centerpiece, and then moved when serving a meal.

display/photo by Linda Roberts

Surf's Up! A wooden serving dish became the base for this Hawaiian display.

display/photos
by Barbara
Westberg

Barbara Westberg's 2013 base was a 15.75" wooden serving platter with a 1.25" lip. She had purchased the Season's Bay "Sandy Beach" last summer to use in her 2012 vignette, but the base couldn't contain the sand. She had been searching ever since.

She began by cutting a 13.5" circle from a remnant of blue plastic water from LeMax®. This was laid in the platter as the base for the rest of the scene. The Snow Village *Moondoggie's Board Shop* was placed on top of the "water". Lighting was provided by the Department56® *Display Anywhere Lighting Retrofit Unit*. She did not include the transmitter piece, to turn on this house only. Because of the lip on the platter, she was able to easily hide the button.

Behind the shop, she placed three Fontanini® palm trees. In front of the shop, she placed the coordinating Snow Village piece *Beachside Christmas,* plus an older Snow Village piece - *A Day At The Beach*.

Last, she sprinkled the Season's Bay *Sandy Beach* which includes various miniature seashells in the back, sides and a small amount in the front to complete the setting.

They say "Diamonds are a Girl's Best Friend". However, Sue Chretien thought it was much more fun to have her own jewelry store! The Brightsmith Jeweler to the Queen building from Dickens' Village was placed on a decorative mirror. She placed a large faux diamond purchased from a craft store, and then raided her jewelry box for costume jewelry, pearls, rhinestones, etc. This is an easy display to make. It took longer to get the building out of its box than to set up the vignette. Many craft stores have jewels of varying colors and sizes – make it your own!

Stepping out on the town – was Jeff Chretien's idea for a snappy display geared to the guys, but still as appealing to women. A white tuxedo shirt, black top hat, walking stick and shiny patent leather dress shoes, compliment the University Club and the Regal Ballroom.

- They're Quick & Easy -

display/photo by Sue Chretien

display/photo by Jeff Chretien

Neutral colored candle holders, blending with the tones of
the wooden box provide a setting for a candle themed building.

display/photo by Sue Henne

- Antique Candle Holders
Enhance New England Candle Shop -

Sue Henne has a collection of antique candle holders acquired throughout the years mostly from garage sales. On the right, the tall candle with the black iron wound around it is called a "courting candle". Years ago, a father would time his daughter's suiters visitations by adjusting the length of the candle. The holder on the left has the original wax candle around it, which threads through the horizontal handle when lit. Sue merges some of her candle holder collection with the New England *Platt's Candles & Wax* building resting on a wooden box. The fence and hedge are Department 56®, and the small candle figures are old *"Gurley's"*.

An old wooden Coca Cola® crate was modified by adding a set of wooden wheels and a pull. Styrofoam was used to cover the compartments in the crate which holds the North Pole's Coca Cola® Fizz Factory. Caps from Coca Cola® bottles form a pathway to the building. display/photo by Don Rush

A grouping of Coca Cola® related items form another Coca Cola® themed vignette. display/photo by Frank Mapes

Coca Cola® is one of the world's most recognized brand names. Several villages have licensed designs which have been very popular additions to those villages. There are many products produced carrying the name and logo to group with one or several of the village pieces. Frank Mapes found an old Coca Cola® ice cooler, and added the Christmas in the City *Coca Cola® Soda Fountain*, signs and other accessories into a charming vignette.

– Pick a Theme & Tell a Story . . .

The shipwreck display was based on a real life experience depicted in a movie. *display/photo by Linda Roberts*

The Ship Wreck – A few years ago, Linda Roberts saw the movie about the wreck of the Endurance, which was Sir Ernest Shackleton's ship that became encased in the ice on an expedition to the South Pole. It inspired her to create this shipwreck scene with all the men unloading the boat, and living on the ice berg. She featured the *Emily Louise* from New England Village, and "sunk" it into a large piece of styrofoam. She covered the wreath at the front of the boat with twine and used several Dickens' accessories. One of the men is chopping up a tree, but since there were no trees available at the South Pole, she built a crate around the tree stump using toothpicks. There was a photographer on board the ship. He is documenting the story.

...And/Or, Make Your Own Bases -

Sue Paolello cut styrofoam into shapes such as the mitten and sleigh to the left. Then, she chose a building for each one and accessorized the setting. She advanced the process further when she cut, formed and painted the stylized poinsettia below into a very attractive display. Sue cleverly placed an elf on most of the top petals. They could function as table centerpieces or displayed on an end table. display/photos

by Sue Paolello / Carol

Chapter 7:
- Eat, Drink
& Be Merry -
A Taste for Vignettes
by Sue Chretien

Don't have enough room for all your buildings? Take the food-related buildings into your kitchen or dining room!

The Santa's Sweet Shop Series buildings sit on top of a dining room buffet. Note the picture in the background is even gift wrapped to accent the scene. *display/photo by Sue Chretien*

I have loads of villages! However, when one particular village was launched, I said – *"I just don't have room."* Until however, they came out with this adorable piece that I just had to have. And, that gave birth to doing food-related vignettes in my kitchen and dining room. From a small display (about 20-25 houses) nestled on a buffet or china cabinet, to just a single building elevated on a cake plate or other novel container, you can add fun and whimsy to your kitchen for the holidays; or every day. Just make sure to place your vignettes with care, as you don't want them to

E. Tipler's Wines and Spirits in Dickens Village is a great piece. I love the detail. Since I have an Old World Tuscany look going on in my house, this vignette plays right into it. Set into an apothecary jar is the building and the accessory. I had an additional apothecary jar full of wine corks, and two very jolly Italian chefs serving up holiday cheer. When Christmas is over, the same house and accessory go on to a footed glass cake plate, along with the jar of wine corks, and some faux grapes cascading on either side. It's a quick switch and allows me to enjoy the building year round. display/photo by Sue Chretien

be knocked off their perches, or have cooking greases mar those lovely displays.

Here are some great possibilities: **Glass Containers** – oh, think of the possibilities! Glass containers are great for making vignettes. A footed cake plate elevates your building or buildings to a new level, and gives them an air of importance. Add a styrofoam base, or fabric, glass tiles, a sheet of small tiles from your home improvement store, moss, or just leave it bare, and you've got the beginnings of a great vignette. For instance, during the Christmas Holidays, in my kitchen, I have *Fretta's Fruit Cake Company* displayed on a small covered cake dish, I added a couple of ribbon bows to the top of the cover, as well as, to the base. It is pictured on page 99. Instant charm.

Apothecary Jars are another great container, and it keeps

Couple E. Tipler with a French Restaurant also serving Wine and Spirits. The duo can be placed into a curio cabinet or book-case, as well as, in the kitchen. Pair with glass decators or fancy wine, champagne or martini glasses - filled for special occasions, or not. display/photo by Mary Jewell

your building or large accessory protected so it can be placed any-where. Fill up the bottom with rocks, snow, faux fruit, nuts, until it is at the right height and level, and set your house inside, add a tree or two (or floral picks that are more flat if room is tight). Add accessories. And, replace the lid. You're done - until you change it.

A large beverage dispenser was used to display the Smoking Bishop from Dickens' Village. Fit the building to the size, shape and feel of the container. It can easily be changed by the season or event. display/photo by Ellen Somerwill

Bell jars come in numerous styles, sizes and shapes. This one measures approximately 12" in diameter and is about 18" tall. Although this one is not food related, any cherished building can be showcased, while being protected from the elements behind glass. A small platform was shaped to fit the bottom of this jar and colored in tones of brown and green, with small blue aquarium stones representing the flowing river. If you want a new look, remove this building and substitute another. The bell jar doesn't take up much room, so it can be placed almost anywhere.

display/photo by Ray Bukovszky

Linda Roberts is constantly on the look out for interesting accents to couple with her village pieces. The above cloche vignettes feature miniature ornaments. Find color coordinated picks and ribbons to dress it up. display/photos by Linda Roberts

▶
▶
▶
▶   **Large beverage dispensers** are also another way to display as seen in Ellen Somerwill's vignette on page 96. You can use this for whatever season or holiday, change out the base, the building, and you have one hard working vessel that will give you an awesome vignette.

Cloches are a bell shaped glass cover that were originally used for protecting plants from cold temperatures. But now, they have a new purpose, and that is to augment your village vignette.

Crystal, Etched or Cut Glass: Do you have any beautiful crystal or glass serving dishes, bowls, platters, etc. that you never use? Many families pass them down through the generations.

A four-shelf étagère makes a perfect spot for a vignette and you could theme it however you like. It only takes up 14 square inches, and gives vertical height. Although the tile on the shelves didn't exactly lend itself to snow, some foam craft sheets fixed that right up. The light cords were kept tidy by using white twist-ties down the vertical length of one of the supports to the shelf in the back. Top it with ribbons and voila!

Instant gratification! Looks great, too! displays/ photos by Sue Chretien

My grandmother always made fruitcake during the holidays. Look how delightful Fretta's Fruit Cake Company looks under glass. Add a small sprinkling of snow, and the accessory piece. Holiday memories revisited!

These are great pieces for developing vignettes and will show off your crystal or heirlooms, as well. Start looking through your china cabinet! And, be on the search for suitable pieces at thrift stores, and other second hand venues.

Interesting containers and how they relate to the building, along with fun decorative items to enhance the vignette, and a little imagination are all that you need to pull this off. The vignettes in this chapter are sure to spark your imagination.

So what do you do with all of those empty baskets taking up space in your closet? Well, make a village vignette, of course! This delightful basket is filled with floral foam, cut to fit the basket, then topped with a 1" piece of styrofoam cut to fit just slightly below the lip of the basket. I used Christmas Bread Bakers from North Pole, added a few elves, and some faux bread, obtained from a local craft store, and hot glued a bamboo

skewer to each to insert them into the styrofoam behind the house. Add a couple of bows to the side of the basket, and some charming baking Santa's for a great effect. This sits on top of my refrigerator, another overlooked place to display village vignettes!

display/photo by Sue Chretien

Similarly done to the vignette above, these Merry Makers are rolling out dough, baking pies and bread for the holidays. Instead of styrofoam for the top, peel and stick tiles from a local home improvement store were used, to look like the floor in these jolly monk's kitchen. *display/photo by Sue Chretien*

Pedestal serving plates provide different elevations for this North Pole setting. Holiday ribbon repeats the coloration in the buildings, while the trees give a strong vertical contrast. Display Anywhere Lighting is a wonderful invention for a quick set-up. display/photo by Susie Clough O'Brien

- *For My Sweet Tart* -

Each of the villages has many restaurants and places to eat, as well as, many buildings related to food. They can individually be showcased using their theme as *THE* theme of the vignette.

Bakeries are particularly popular. Every village has at least one. Elements that can be used with them are also plentiful.

■ *Bakers:* There are numerous stylized figures available. Older antique varieties, selections of collectible designs or inexpensive knock-offs can all be used. Most of them are much larger in scale than the village accessories, but that only adds to the appeal, intrigue and uniqueness of the village centered collage.

■ *Utensils & Gadgets:* Look through Grandma's kitchen. Wooden rolling pins, cookie sheets, cookie cutters. Thrift stores probably have many discards that could be repurposed into a charming vignette.

Barbara Benjamin loves doing kitchen and food related vignettes, especially during the Holidays. The two displays on these pages are her designs! She utilized the Starbucks Coffee and Krispy Kreme Donut Shop buildings with their accessories and props on the back counter. She also created the beautiful Christmas basket appearing on pages 76-77. display/photo by Barbara Benjamin

Christmas Bread Bakers and Elsie's Gingerbread houses from North Pole are displayed on a butcher block table along with corresponding cook books to further the baking theme. Or, take any of the other bakeries. Add some cookie cutters or ornaments. There are a lot of ornaments related to cupcakes, slices of cake, cookies, etc. Obtain some miniature baking utensils. Be creative! Look for related items that can be paired with your favorite building(s)!

display/photo by Barbara Benjamin

■ ***Faux Food:*** Check out your local craft store for replicas of actual food - breads, cookies, cupcakes, grapes and other appropriate items for your particular display.

Another approach is to develop a "restaurant row" featuring numerous ethnic restaurants on top of the kitchen cabinets. At a higher elevation, they would not need much detailing, but they could be accented with larger colorful bottles picking up the colors in the building(s), decorative boxes or related items. At lower levels, detailing is more visible, thus more important. Combine fish netting with a seafood restaurant; or a Chinese lantern, chop sticks and fortune cookies with *Wong's in Chinatown*. Menus from local real restaurants of the same ethnicity can form backdrops and/or

The red and green of this festive Christmas Holidays display is depicted in the choice of buildings - Kringle's Korner and the Peppermint House. The gingerbread characters repeat the colors which are complimented by the red wall in Mary Jewell's kitchen display. display/photo by Mary Jewell

items associated with that culture can be included into a stunning vignette. Refer back to the oriental displays on page 80.

Instead of restaurants, substitute a somewhat similar genre. There are numerous pubs in Dickens' Village and taverns in Christmas In The City. Pubs and taverns can decorate a kitchen or home bar setting and/or lend themselves to a St. Patrick's Day theme. Add a few bottles of your favorite brew/spirits. Include some with interesting labels obtained on your world travels. Mix in several with exotic shapes and colors, or unique decanters or glassware. Get those decorative beer steins out of storage. Couple them with Alpine pieces or breweries. There are so many possibilities.

Pick a building or several. Determine what would have a logical pairing, then look for those items. Or, do the reverse. Locate an interesting object to feature, then seek a suitable building. *Remember when the hunt was part of the fun of village collecting? It can be again!* Creativity equals great vignettes!

Debbie Shelgren placed her Santa's Paper Snowflake Studio into an over-sized cup. The size of the building allows for some accent trees; and the colors of the cup coordinate with the building tones. This small vignette could fit almost anywhere!
display/photo by Debbie Shelgren

The North Pole Cranberry House is the focal point of the vignette by Jeff and Mary Jo Lawson. Mary Jo made trees out of Popcorn Balls, a sidewalk out of popcorn kernals, and the snow out of popped popcorn. *display/photo by Jeff and Mary Jo Lawson*

- *The Thought Process is Important!* -

■ *A theater shows movies. Most villages have one. Select a theater from your favorite village!* (Check!)

■ *Movies were shot with a movie camera. Attic? Thrift Store? Find one!* (Check!)

■ *Movie film used to come in reels. Ditto.* (Check!)

■ *Movie posters or DVD covers are not hard to find. (Internet or brick & mortar stores)* (Check!)

■ *Popcorn is eaten in a theater as viewers are watching the movie. (Microwave a batch.)* (Check!)

■ *Put the elements together! You are done! Enjoy!*

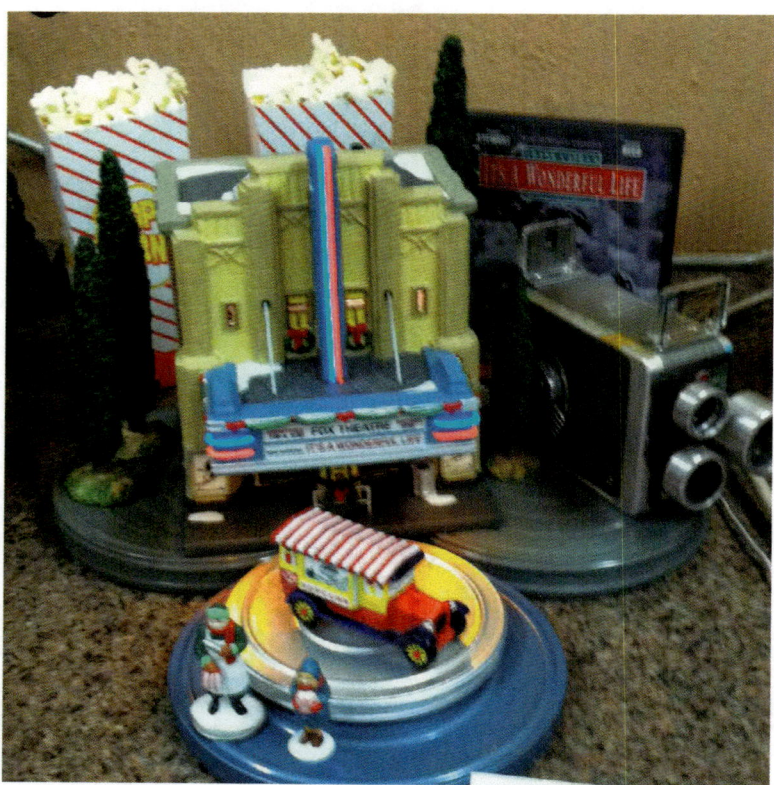

For an "any time" display, take a theater from any village, add a couple of vintage movie reel tins to place the theater on as the base, then add people going to the theater. In this instance, I enhanced the vignette by adding the DVD of the movie shown on the marquee and added a couple containers of popcorn. Very Quick! Very Easy! Very Impressive! display/photo by Sue Chretien

Anne Saxe uses the top of an antique cabinet which measures 45" wide x 9" deep. It can easily be changed as desired. Her southwestern display including the older SV Palos Verdes House, Spanish Mission Church, Rosita's Cantina, and she later added the LeMax® Taco Shop after she located it. Palm trees, vehicles and accessories complete the scene.

display/photo by Anne Saxe

- *Use the Space above Cabinets and Hutches* -

These higher places are out of the way, thus much detailing is ineffective, but they do work well for creating a themed display such as a restaurant row or combining village pieces with larger unrelated items like baskets, pottery, figures or greenery.

Chapter 8

- Holidays -
Throughout the Year

In Bob Bogart's story, the upper shelf of a bookcase holds the home of his happy couple... *display/photo by Bob Bogart*

Valentine's Day -

*T*hroughout the year, there are several smaller holidays that can easily be subjects of village vignettes. Valentine's Day has several Snow Village pieces featured on the next several pages. Some buildings from other villages can also be substituted if you want to take some creative liberties. Dickens', Christmas In The City and Snow Village have Irished themed - or other suitable - buildings for celebrating St. Patrick's Day. Don't forget the numerous Dickens' Village Pubs to accent a March display. An Easter church or a visit from the Easter Bunny can make an excellent vignette. And, there are also numerous buildings that can be used for the Fourth of July. *(See pages 58-59.)* Halloween will be covered in a later chapter.

In 2002, Department 56 introduced the first of several Snow Village buildings in a subseries known as Celebrate Love. There are four buildings in this set, all of which were retired in 2005 or 2006. Bob Bogart developed two vignettes on a small bookcase, around Valentine's Day. They were easy to develop, and Bob feels like it is a good way to enjoy the hobby in the "off-season".

The Plan

The first step in constructing this display was planning the layout of the buildings and accessories. Color was not involved in the decision, as all four buildings are in the red, white and pink color palette. Bob decided that the lower shelf of the bookcase would hold three buildings and one accessory, with the unifying theme of the courtship and wedding of the happy couple. On this level were *Cupid's Card Shop*, the *Sweetheart Candy Shop*, and the *Chapel of Love*. This last piece includes *The Happy Couple* accessory, which was also displayed in this vignette. The thought pattern was to envision a young man buying a Valentine's Card for his intended, progressing to buying gifts for his sweetheart, and ultimately, popping the question and getting married.

On the upper shelf, *Hearts & Blooms Cottage* and its accessory, *Young Love*, would show the home of the happy couple, and to the side, a young boy giving a push to a young girl on a swing. Are they brother and sister born to this happy couple, or as the accessory name seems to indicate, young boyfriend and girlfriend, ready to repeat the cycle of love?

Preparing the Backdrop

Bob began this display with the backdrop. He carefully measured the width and height (shelf to shelf) of the bookcase, cut a piece of foam-core to the appropriate size, and then wrapped it with a Valentine's Day gift-wrap. He added a small opening - large enough for wires and plugs to pass through - in a spot that would not be visible when the display was complete.

Next, he measured the depth of the display, accounting for the

...while the lower shelf above depicts the courtship.

display/photo by Bob Bogart

thickness of the foam-core back piece, and repeated the wrapping procedure on the two sidepieces. An online search for antique Valentine's Day cards provided printouts, which were attached to the sides and backdrop. *(Hint: if you are looking for online images, search for large, high resolution images so that when you print them, they are clear and not pixelized or blurry).* Bob found a lighted *Heart and Arrow* at a local craft store, and attached it to the back piece with dabs of hot glue, making certain it was placed close to the top of the background piece. These steps (except for the Heart and Arrow light) were repeated for the upper shelf.

Construction of the Vignettes

Starting with the back piece, Bob placed it firmly against the back of the bookcase. There was no need to use a fastener, as the sidepieces, once in place, held it firmly in position. He threaded the wires from the Heart and Arrow through the openings, and guided the wire to its outlet. The sidepieces were put into position, again held in place by friction. At this point, he carefully measured the width and depth of the display areas, and transferred those measurements to styrofoam. Using a *Hot Wire Foam Factory*® Scroll Table, He carefully cut the bases for the two vignettes, and test fit them in the display. The scroll table is not a necessity – any foam-cutting tool will do the job. Bob used it, as he has worked with it before and knew it would give smooth, straight edges.

Because of the small size of these displays, Bob opted not to have any elevation changes, as they would be difficult to accomplish in such a small area. On the lower vignette, he placed the three buildings in an arc, as this gives more visual interest than if they were in a straight line. Once satisfied with the building placement, he traced their outlines on the styrofoam and removed them so he could prepare the base.

Using a marker, Bob drew the location of sidewalks and grassy areas onto the base. Starting with the grassy areas (he chose grass rather than snow) were added to provide some additional color to the display, The foam was treated with a slightly diluted

Valentine's Day –

white glue (Elmer's), and sprinkled with Woodland Scenics® ground foam, using a green blend to better approximate winter grass. He added some yellow blend and burnt grass blend to the grassy area and allowed the area to partially dry. Using a large medicine dropper, he dripped diluted white glue to fasten everything securely. Shrubs were prepared by taking a clump of lichen from a model train store. The clumps were sprayed with hairspray, and more ground foam was sprinkled over the clumps. He uses the cheapest pump bottle hairspray he can find. When dry, he sprayed it again, and sprinkled on some additional colored ground foam. In this display, Bob used red ground foam to represent blossoms on the shrubs - Artistic liberty: even if Valentine's Day is in February! *Some parts of the country do have pretty blossoms in February!*

Once the grassy areas were dry, Bob coated the white sidewalk areas with the white glue solution, and carefully placed red foil hearts (from a crafts store) and allowed the display to dry. Hearts Garland was attached to the front edge of the foam for the lower display with hot glue. For the upper display, he used foam "Candy Hearts" to decorate the front edge of the foam.

Putting it Together

The bases were placed on the bookcase, and the buildings in their appropriate spots. Wires were routed through the openings in the back of the display and plugged in. He made no attempt to hide the wires, as they are not visible when viewing the display. Bob, then, added the landscaping – trees, shrubs, and a few mini-accessories such as the flower pots in front of the *Hearts and Blooms Cottage*. Adding the accessories completed this tribute to love!

The Valentine Snow Village buildings used in these vignettes are all retired, but if you do not have them, substitute other buildings such as jewelry stores, flower shops, chocolate or candy shops, card shops, churches or another buildings that is associated with Cupid, St. Valentine or romance.

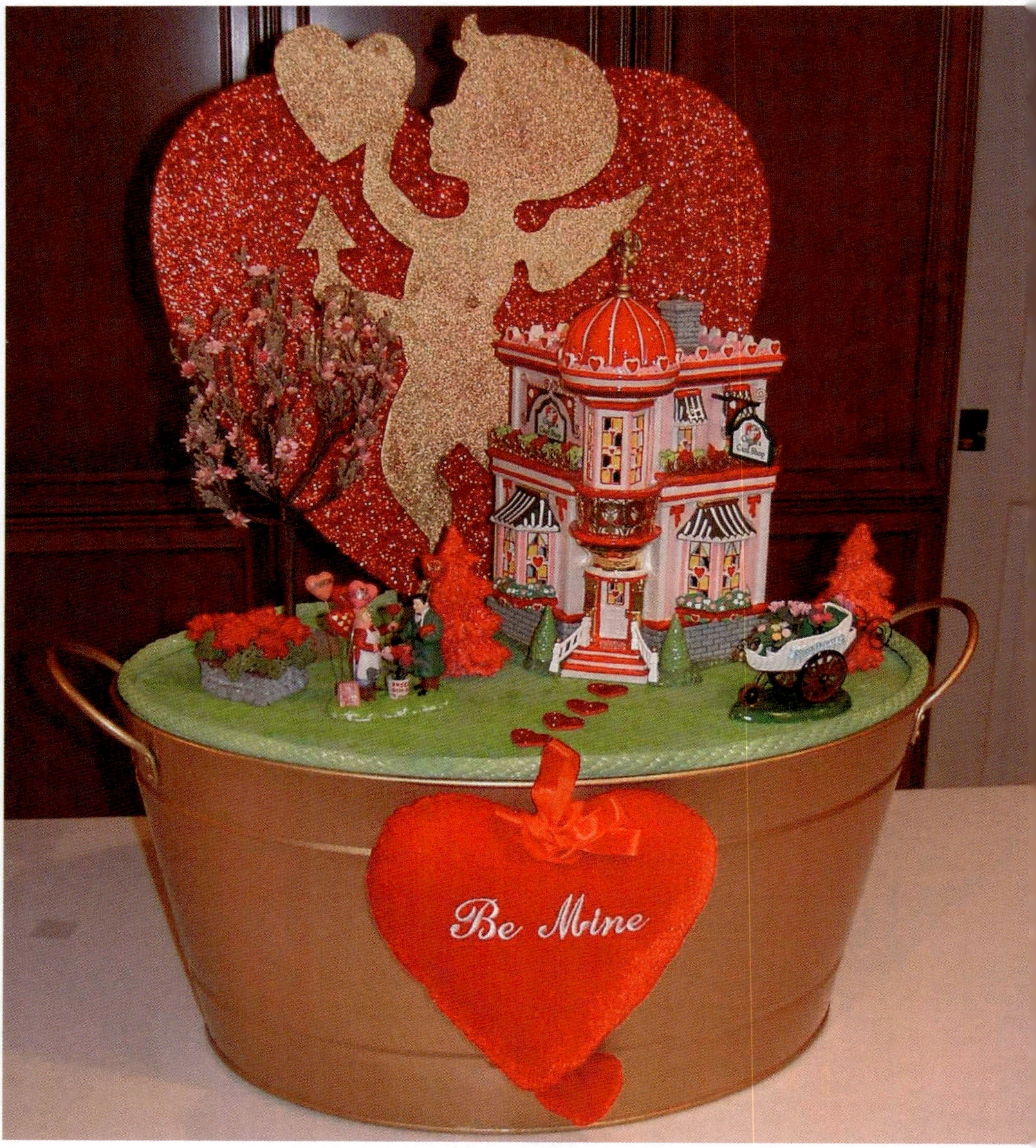

Valentine's Day -

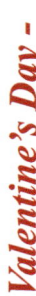

A copper tub makes a fabulous base for many vignettes. The copper color ties the tub and the cupid together within the overall display. The heart can also be angled slightly for another dramatic effect! *display/photo by Robert and Sharon Cone*

- Add Cupid to a Valentine's Day Vignette -
Coordinate the colors with the container.

This Valentine display was constructed for a vignette contest at a village club meeting. Robert and Sharon Cone wanted an interesting base to begin the construction. They found a copper colored wine tub at a local home goods type store. A piece of 3/4" styrofoam was laid over the opening and traced to determine the display base. A hot wire knife was used to trim the oval to the correct size to fit snuggly in the top of the tub. Some additional 2" foam rectangles were place inside the tub to act as a foundation since the building was quite heavy. The oval was not as perfect as desired so Robert took a piece of white nylon rope and covered the outside edge with a section of the rope. The styrofoam and the rope were then glued together and painted light green with spray paint. Some green ground foam from his model railroad supplies was sprinkled on the green paint while it was still wet to add a grassy texture and to mottle the green tones.

They decided to use *Cupids Card Shop* as the center piece of the display, plus they added *For Your Sweetheart*, and *Fresh Flower Cart* as accessories. Some LeMax® trees were used to add landscaping. A spring tree with pink flowers and two white trees from a Christmas display were used. The white trees were spray painted red to add to the Valentine theme. A small heart shaped planter - on the left side of the display was cut from foam and sprayed grey. Some small red flowers from a craft store were "planted in it". Red hearts for the pathway were obtained from a scrap booking department of a craft store. To finish the display a large red heart and cupid were used from a party store as the backdrop. If the colors need to be changed to coordinate better with the colors in the vignette, paint them. There are numerous tones to match, and, there are several colors of glitter available if the intent is to make them sparkle.

Around Valentine's Day, there are many heart shaped boxes available. Some are only made of cardboard, but fancier ones can be found adorned in materials such as shiny satins or beautiful brocades. Some are large enough to hold a building. Some are offered in a variety of sizes which can then be stacked or utilized artistically as either the base of the vignette, a back drop or in conjunction with another type of container. Possibilities are endless!

Valentine's Day -

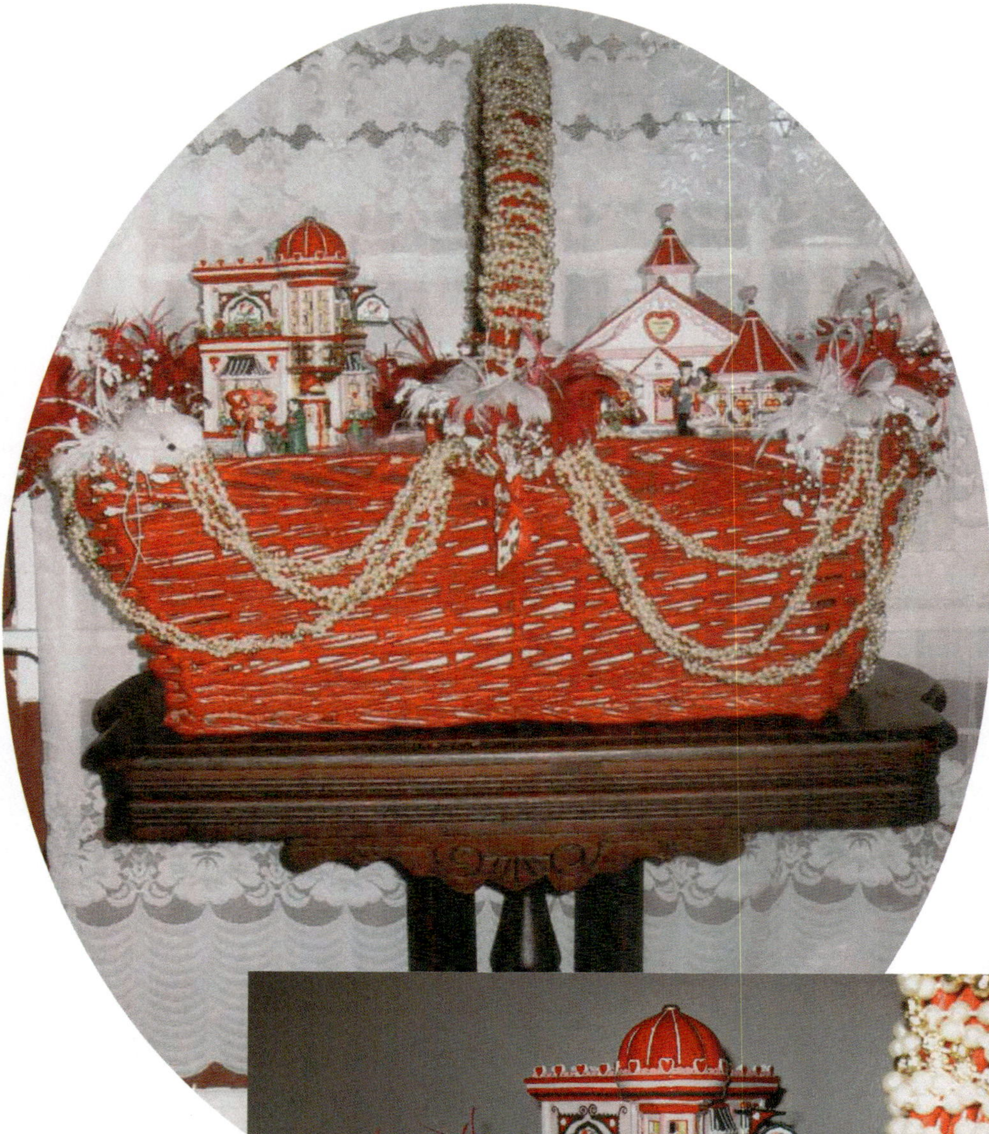

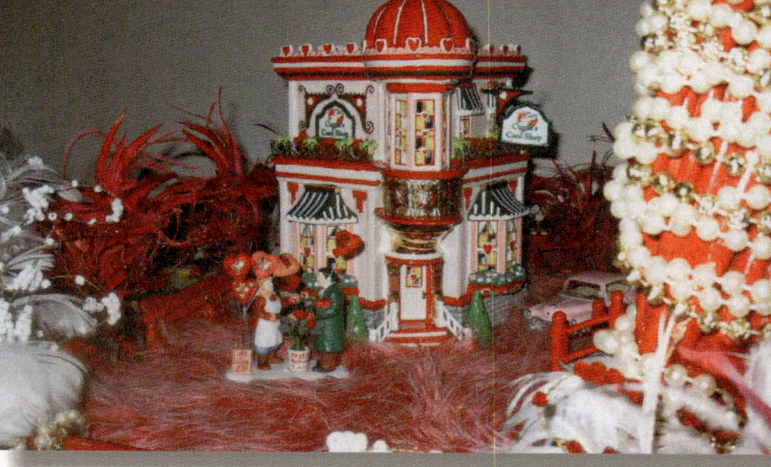

display/photos by Gail Garbo

- *A Victorian Valentine's Celebration* -

This Valentine's display features the Snow Village "Chapel of Love" and "Cupid's Cardshop", as well as the CIC "For Your Valentine" accessory. It also includes a mauve fur fabric and feather floral picks, in addition to pearl beads, and the heart-shaped candy box. The red bridge was found at a pet store.

display/photos by Gail Garbo

Gail Garbo found a perfect basket to create a Valentine's Day vignette. It was large and it was red! What else does one need? She cut a piece of styrofoam with a hot wire to fit inside, then cut some fur fabric to cover the styrofoam. The fabric was secured with metal floral picks. The houses and accessories were positioned. The feather floral picks were added to the basket. Strands of pearl beads were placed throughout the vignette - and under the bridge - to represent water. More wrapped the handle, and draped around the basket. The last thing that was added was the small heart shaped candy box on the front of the basket. The construction time was about one hour to assemble this attractive vignette.

display/photos by Anita Poitras

We all have a wee bit of Irish in us . . . especially on St. Patrick's Day . . . .

Winter's snow will soon be melting and thoughts go to Spring: and St. Patrick's Day. Anita Poitras created an Irish St. Patrick's Day Parade on her coffee table. She mixed two Christmas in the City buildings and the souvenir kiosk from Snow Village with accessories from both villages.

Green sparkles and a few Shamrocks provide more atmosphere, plus a very slight amount of snow has been added since it is not uncommon for snow to fall in Montreal before or during the St. Patrick's Day Parade.

The first recorded St. Patrick's Day parade was not held in Ireland, but in New York City - March 17, 1762.

- Green Dominates: St. Patrick's Day -

There are several buildings suitable to develop a St. Patrick's Day vignette. Whether a single piece or multiple pieces are used, the day can be celebrated in style! display/photo by Robert Cone

Robert Cone used *Molly O' Brien's Irish Pub* for his St. Patrick's Day vignette. He started with two pieces of 3/4" styrofoam. One was painted sky blue for the backdrop and the other was painted in a light tan for the base. The pub was placed in the middle of the tan piece. A section of highway and a brick walkway were used for the road and sidewalk in front of the pub. The *St. Patrick's Village Express Truck,* a 1935 Dusenberg, and *Serving Irish Ale* were selected for accessories. A piece of grass mat from a model railroad store and a selection of trees were used behind and around the sides of the pub.

The most difficult part of the display was the rainbow, which Robert made out of colored paper. He used a homemade compass: *translation* - a thumb tack on a piece of string with a pencil on the other end, to layout the radius for the curves. Although a relatively simple display, it's perfect for the March festivities!

Easter display/photos by Joe Meyers

- Easter & Pastels Colors:
Eggs are Just Part of this Holiday -

This fabulous Easter display was done by Joe Meyers for a display contest. Their club display contest is usually in the Spring, and he wanted to do something that was colorful and cheery. Thus, he made this egg out of sugar and a skein of multi-colored pastel yarn. Growing up, his Grandmother would make these eggs and put little Easter scenes inside them. He remember looking through the hole in the egg with amazement at the scene she created in the delicate egg. Of course, the grandchildren were never allowed to touch them. Making this egg was a wonderful way to bring back some memories from his childhood.

Finding a balloon big enough to wrap sugar coated string around it was a challenge. He settled for a big mylar balloon, which wasn't perfect, but it worked.

A friend, David Rineair, whose vignette appears on page 131, helped him. The down side is that

Fur fabric hides the rough edges of the opening.

Easter - Egg Theme

sugar was everywhere: on the kitchen table, on their clothes, on the floor and on his dog. He remembers still picking sugar out of his dog's coat for weeks afterward.

The Snow Village *Flower Shop* was chosen as the focal point because it was a building that reminded Joe of Easter; plus, it was the right size to fit into the egg. The accessory used was *The Girl and The Goose*.

After the sugar dried, the balloon was popped and a hole was cut to accommodate the interior display. He set the egg on a styrofoam base coated with the woodland scenics grass, which rested on a paper towel cardboard roll. Easter grass was used to fill in around the sides and in the interior. The building, accessory, and a tree with eggs hanging from it were placed inside. The cut edges were covered with fur fabric to hide any irregularities and sharper edges. The egg was adorned with an Easter Egg themed ribbon.

Moss was glued on the base to make it look like the egg was sitting on grass. Birds, birds nests, and butterflies were added to make it look more like Spring. Although it is not a quick and easy display, it was fun to do, and it turned out beautiful. Smaller eggs can also be made for Snow Bunnies, or smaller scenes.

- A Pastel Colored Church Makes a Simple, yet Effective Vignette -

The *Happy Easter Church* is ideal for an Easter vignette. Merge the church and the accessory pieces with pastel flowers so abundant in Spring. Blue (roof color) and orange (flower color) are complimentary colors, Thus, tints and hues of the color duo make attractive combinations. Or, the more classic white gardenias, accented with the blue candles coordinating with the blues in the church are also attractive. If this church is unavailable, many others in the more pastel pallette can also be featured. Since many parts of the country can still be under a blanket of snow, it matters not if there are snow patches on the roofs. The flowers can cover some of them, or create some snow patches on the base of the display to blend them into the setting.

Easter - Religious Themes

A very simple Easter vignette is made with the Snow Village Happy Easter Church, its accessory pieces, and pastel or Spring-time silk flowers. Change the flowers for a more solumn feel and add some candles. It takes more time to light the candles than it did to set up the display. displays/photos by Leigh Gieringer

- *Feature Snowbunnies in an Easter Vignette* -

Snow Babies and Snowbunnies are small compared to most village pieces, thus they can fit into smaller scaled accent pieces like the bird cage pictured here. Add Easter grass for color - matching any color theme desired, several decorative eggs, especially the smaller painted ones, and some complimentary Spring or Easter themed ribbon. In about five minutes, you are done! If you wish to increase the size, similar items, glass serving pieces, candle holders or some related items of varying heights can be added. Place more bunnies nearby.

There are many Snowbunnies from which to choose to add into a bird cage or lantern.
display/photo by Leigh Gieringer

Plastic versions of clay pots provide an intriguing design element to accompany a spring vignette including several Snowbunnies. The pots come in various sizes providing further artistic liberties. Identical arches were cut out of the largest pot allowing the items in the display to be placed within the interior for more display area.

The arch frames the scene. Add some Easter decorations for more color and atmosphere.

display/photos by Ellen Somerwill

- *Another Excellent Spring Theme is a Vignette for Mother's Day.* -

ABOVE: Mother's Day cards make an interesting backdrop for this vignette. RIGHT: The seated figures are G-scaled figures made by Preiser®. The table and chairs were found at a Collector's Gathering. display/photos by Bob Bogart

Bob Bogart constructed this vignette for a club demonstration. He had planned the year so that there would be a display for each month of the club year, showing members that collectors are not just limited to the Christmas Season for displaying villages. Each month, an appropriate Holiday or event was chosen, and a display was built to represent that day. For May, the natural choice was Mother's Day.

Spring: Mother's Day -

The Plan

Often, for Mother's Day, Moms are treated to a nice restaurant meal. Bob decided to choose that idea to construct a simple vignette, using *Juliette's School of French Cuisine* (Snow Village) as the restaurant of choice. It would feature an outdoor dining area with spring landscaping. He located an unfinished wooden tea tray that would serve as the vignette's container. He also found a set of figures that would populate the scene in a train store. These figures were from Preiser® Figures, in G Scale. A recent online search shows a similar set, called *Seated Parents with Babies*. This is not the set he used, as there is no older woman to represent Mom. It is possible that Mom was a separate item.

Constructing the Vignette

Juliette's is a brick building, with red and blue trim. Thus, the decision was made to paint the tea tray in the blue family, but Bob chose a pastel color, so the tray would accent, not dominate the scene. A styrofoam base was cut to fill the tea tray. After placing the building on the display area, he traced its outline once he was happy with its position. He placed it at an angle to the front of the tea tray, as that orientation is more interesting to the viewer. Removing the building, he sketched out the rest of the scene. In front of the restaurant would be a flagstone dining area. A small pond was placed near the back of the scene, and a grassy area was created in front of the pond.

Using foam-carving tools, Bob first removed a thin area where the pond would be located, and the flagstones were carved into the surface. This area was painted, first with a black paint. The goal here was to get dark shadows between the flagstones forming the grout lines. Once that was dry, a brownish-gray paint was applied. To retain the dark areas between the flagstones, he made certain his brush was not overloaded with paint, and kept the brush flat with the surface. The gray paint did not get into the cracks. Next, he painted the grassy area with green latex paint to prevent the styrofoam from dissolving. While it was still wet, he sprinkled the area with a grass-green ground foam. After the area dried, he dripped on a slightly diluted white glue mixture to ensure that the ground foam was securely fastened, and allowed it to dry.

Bob painted the pond area, again with latex or acrylic paints. The banks of the pond were painted an earth brown, and the pond bottom was painted a dark blue. When the paint was dry, he carefully poured in a thin layer of Realistic Water® from Woodland Scenics®. This material can be built up in thin layers, but must cure between successive pourings. If waves are desired, a similar product called Water Effects® is also available from Woodland Scenics®.

Surrounding the pond are flowers that were constructed from various colored artificial floral stems. He used floral stems that represent just budding plants. The individual bud cluster was pulled off of the stem, and half of a toothpick was pushed into the center hole where the cluster was attached to the stem. The toothpick allowed the newly created flower to be "planted" into the styrofoam.

The Spring flowering bushes are clumps of lichen (found at train stores). The clump was sprayed with hairspray from a pump bottle, and then sprinkled with ground foam. Bob started with green, re-sprayed the shrub, and added the pink or lavender ground foam to finish off the flowering shrub.

The blooming tree in the vignette was made from a Department 56® *Bare Branch Tree*. Another model railroad product, Poly Fiber® was stretched and pulled out so it was light and airy, and then attached to the tree using tacky glue. This served as the surface on which ground foam adhered. He sprayed the Poly Fiber® with the hairspray, and sprinkled on some ground foam. When that was done and dried, he re-sprayed the tree to make everything hold together better.

Setting up the Vignette

Once the construction phase was completed, it took only a few minutes to finish the vignette. A *Display Anywhere Lighting*

Spring: Mother's Day -

Retrofit Unit was installed, so that no cord to an outlet was needed, and the building was placed on the display. The trees and shrubs were added, followed by the tables and the family. Bob found that for stability, the tables and the figures needed a little help. He used Tacky Wax® to attach the figures to the chairs, and a tiny dab of hot glue to the legs of the table and chairs. Small potted plants, found at a Village Gathering, were added to the tables as center-pieces. As Mother's Day cards arrived, they were displayed around the vignette, to serve as a backdrop.

Using a computer, Bob printed out a small sign that is attached to the Juliette's signboard that came with the building as an accessory. The new sign helps to tie this display to the specific event that is being represented.

After Mother's Day has passed, all components are stored together in a box. For future Mother's Days, it will take only min-utes to set up the vignette, to be enjoyed all over again.

- Use Color to Define the Season -

Spring, with its abundant new growth of flowering trees, bushes and other plants, is a colorful and memorable time of year. Any number of buildings, whether there are snow patches or not, can be showcased.

display/photo by Bob Eustice

Seasonal - Spring -

The Sweetbriar Cottage fits nicely into the hand made shadow box. It was constructed from styrofoam and framed with a wooden picture frame. display/photo by Bob Eustice

The inspiration for this display came from Thomas Kinkade's cottage paintings. This display made by Bob Eustice features the Dickens' Village *Sweetbriar Cottage* and *Sweet Roses* accessory. The *Animated Swan Pond* was also incorporated. Additional accessories included the deer from the *Woodland Wildlife Animals*; and a miniature dog, squirrel, birds and rabbits. The deciduous trees, pine trees and weeping willow trees, as well as, the flowering bushes were acquired from Scenic Express®. Woodland Scenics® Coarse Foam Turf (Medium Green) was used for the ground cover. The shadow box type enclosure (23" wide, 19" high and 21" deep) was constructed from 1" thick styrofoam sheets. It was painted black on the outside and sky blue on the inside. The picture frame mounted to the front of the enclosure was purchased from a craft store.

Seasonal – Spring –

Obtain one glass, footed cake server, and wrap a pastel flower garland around it. Place the Lillycott Garden Conservatory on it. The spring trees give some height and color. Quick, and beautiful, too! display/photo by Frank Mapes

As an alternative, the Conservatory - or another spring related building - can be surrounded by real plants in a clay dish. Raise the building up by putting it on a piece of styrofoam. Cover the styrofoam with lichen. Find some small leafed plants to surround the building.

display/photos by David Rineair

The china tea set, complete with a spot of tea, merges well with the Chelsea Market Tea Monger and the Joseph Edward Tea Shoppe set on a wooden tray as the occupants meander through the park. *display / photos by Monique Pol*

- *Color Plays a Dominant Role . . .*

If the desire is to develop a Spring vignette, use pastel colors. Light hues of pinks, yellows, violets, blues and greens will typically result in advancing a Spring theme. The tints can be balanced with deeper tones represented in both these displays: the walkway

Make your own container. The square piece of styrofoam becomes the container in this spring vignette by Don Rush. Perfectly cut edges were painted, elevations created, building placed before the vignette was detailed. Instructions to develop the landscaping can be found starting on page 92 in the Realistic Village Vignettes book. display/photos by Don Rush

in the tea related vignette adds depth, while the flowering plum trees in the Season's Bay featuring the *Chapel on the Hill*, add contrast, yet blend with the Spring pastels. Grayed down shades of blues and greens compliment the pastels in a Spring display.

A summer display features more true color. Stronger tones of green, deeper yellows, striking blues - water/skies, but as summer wanes, leaves turn brilliant golds, oranges and reds. Autumn is many collectors' favorite time of year. There is a cornucopia of items that can accent a fall display. And, they are so very colorful!

In addition, numerous harvest related or farming type buildings are available to illustrate an autumn display.

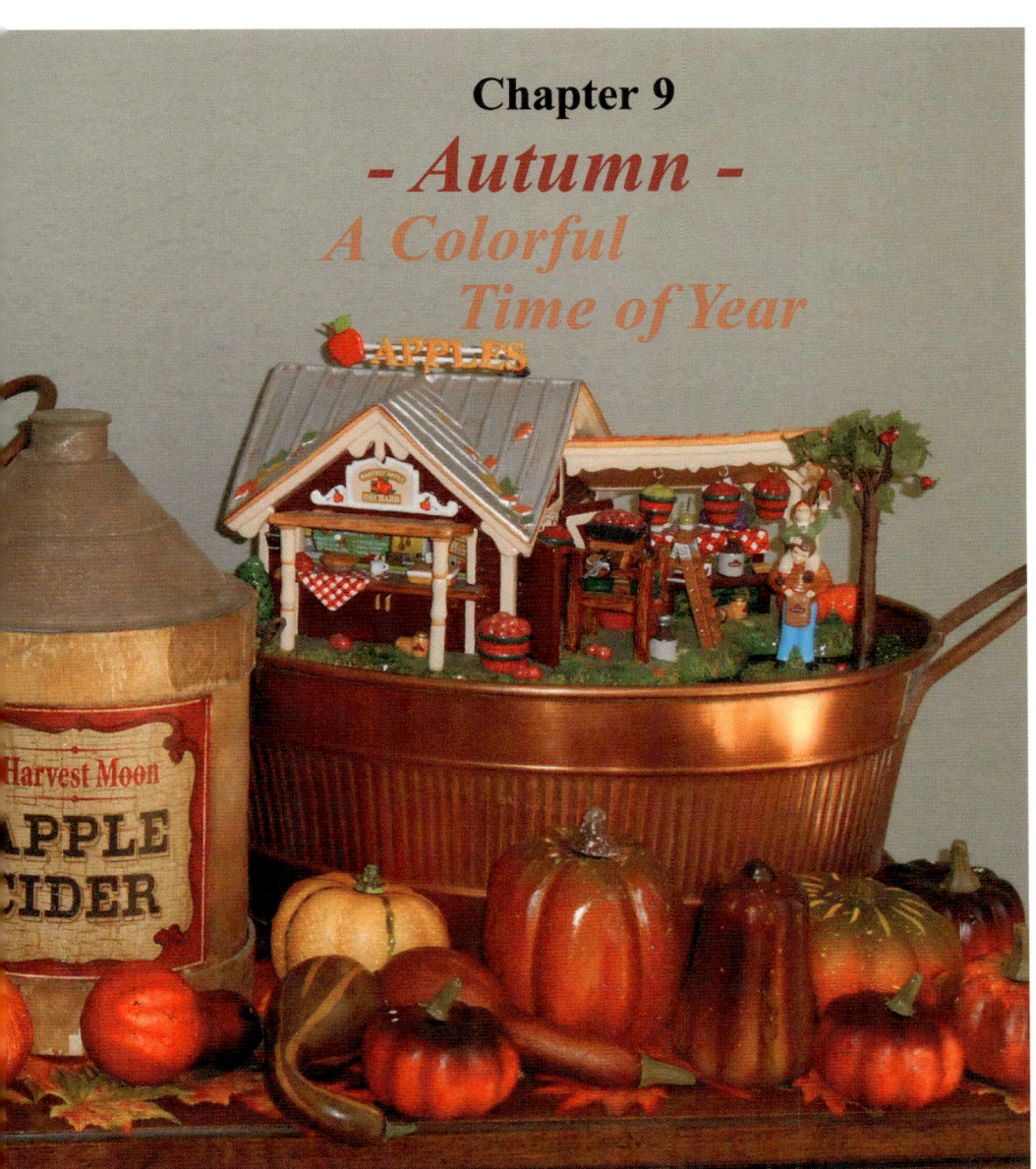

Chapter 9

- *Autumn* -
A Colorful
Time of Year

The copper color of the tubs blends exquisitely with the brilliant autumn colors. Look for copper items to complete other fall displays. display/photo by Frank Mapes

The copper tubs are a natural container to place the Snow Village *Harvest Farm Roadside Sales* and the *Harvest Apple Orchard* pieces. They're supplemented by an old jug for apple cider and several strikingly colorful pumpkins and gourds. All rest on numerous individual artifical maple leaves.

*A labor of love, Mary Ellen McKenna made the fall trees
by hand and thoroughly landscaped her striking autumn table
display.* display/photo by Mary Ellen McKenna

Seasonal - Autumn:

*Mary Jewell placed her autumn display into a bookshelf setting
where she was able to elevate the building and add fall colored
lichen and feature orange-leafed trees.* display/photo by Mary Jewell

Fall pumpkins and leaves dress up the Great Denton Mill.

display/photo by Linda Roberts

Don't fear if you do not have a harvest related building in your collection. Feature a different buildings! Linda Roberts created the above display years ago and brings it out every fall, although it may be accessoried differently each year. New items are available in craft stores, so the atmosphere pieces can be upgraded, switched out, or new additions can be added as desired.

The Dickens' Village _Great Denton Mill_ is placed on a styrofoam circle. She carved it to look like a mill wheel, and sprayed it with gray Fleckstone®. The beige burlap bag is an interesting addition, and blends well with the mill siding. Linda adds lights, pumpkins and other accessories to create a larger display on the top of her Pie Safe cabinet. Since it is small, it can sit almost anywhere!

Jeff McCann located the Applebee's Neighborhood Grill & Bar (the Limited Edition Applebee's 25th Anniversary building). He painted a basket in their corporate colors and cut an opening in the shape of an apple to accommodate an orchard theme within the basket. The building was set on top, accented with fall trees and other accessories.

display/photo
by Jeff McCann

- Spread the Village Virus
by Introducing the Hobby To Non-Villagers -

Robert and Sharon Cone were scheduled to have some non-village friends over. Robert had previously told them about his "village disease". They were unfamiliar with village collecting and displaying. Since it was late September, he would create a Halloween setting to show them what he did in his spare time.

Robert began with a 36" x 72" sheet of styrofoam as the base. He spray painted the foam with varying layers of flat grey, tan, brown, and green in a mottled, uneven pattern, then laid out several buildings randomly until he was satisfied with the layout. Additional pieces of 3/4" and 2" foam were used to raise and highlight some of the buildings. A large lighted Department 56® black tree became the focal point. The buildings used were: *Hauntsburg House, Helga's House of Fortunes, Mickey's Haunted*

Seasonal – Autumn:

TOP: The large D56 tree becomes the focal point of this display. LOWER: This quick and easy vignette started with some fall leaf placemats. The Thanksgiving at Grandmothers and Harvest Farm Roadside Sales houses were featured. The Autumn Landscape, Harvest Bounty, Roadside Produce Stand, and some fall trees were added. Display Anywhere Lighting kits were installed in both houses. displays/photos by Sharon and Robert Cone

House, and *Jack's Pumpkin Carving Studio*. Accessories included: *Ghostly Landscape Set, Haunted Tree House, Strangers Beware, Witch by the Light of the Moon, Harvest Bounty, Happy Haunting, Pumpkin Street Lights*, and the *Caramel Apple Stand*. The most difficult part was the wiring. It was hidden under the raised pieces of foam and adjacent buildings. One place required a sheet of paper painted like the base and camouflaged with lichen and rocks. A thin layer of sand was sprinkled over the surface with some colored lichen. Rocks from the yard completed the display. Dazzled by the display, Robert says: *"I think I spread the 'village virus'."*

Chapter 10:
- Get into the Spirit
of Halloween -

display/photo by John Michael Sanders

display/photo by Randy Vollett

*W*ith each year, Halloween seems to becoming more and more popular. Could it be that there are so many really fabulous buildings, accessories and other pertinent items available? Or, perhaps, it is because our imaginations have gone into overdrive to make overwhelmingly intriguing and fabulous displays? If one has the space, a Halloween Village can be set up, but there are numerous sub-series that are designed to go together if space and the pocketbook are limited.

On pages 140-141, John Michael Sanders has used his mantel to feature the *Shipwreck Lighthouse* and the *Spooky Schooner*, plus two other pieces. His background, painted on a sheet of plywood, and mounted to the wall, ties the display together. Since it is so realistic, this one was also highlighted in *Realistic Village Vignettes,* with a further explanation on how it was done. However, each side could become a vignette on its own merit. Add other Halloween related props to the buildings to stylize it further. Some suggestions can be taken from many of displays that follow.

Some Halloween collectors center their displays around the Grimsley pieces - there are several, a railroad theme, and now a western theme. Because there are numerous pieces, just pick one or two - or more - favorites to build a vignette around it - or them!

Halloween vignettes are Randy Vollett's passion. He truly enjoys searching for unique props to include into his wonderful displays. An example is shown in his Hilda's Nook vignette featuring *Hilda's Witch Haunt*, pictured on the previous page. The hutch, table and books are all made from styrofoam with wood beads for the feet and drawer knobs. The paint is a water base acrylic using a dry brush antique technique. The Ouija board and bottles were purchased at estate sales. The bottles are filled with different textured items, and are all colored in the tones seen within the building. The display measures 21.5"x21.5"x26". Surrounding it are candles, skulls, witches and more. A garland of grape leaves and grapes - the purple color in the building - entwined in a string of lights, ties the vignette together. What an awesome display! Several detailed pictures follow on the next two pages!

These incredible books were hand carved from styrofoam, then meticulously painted to resemble century old volumes.

- The Colors in the Building are Repeated Throughout this Dynamic Vignette -

Numerous unique bottles collected from estate sales were filled with various items. Hues within them coordinate to the colors on the Ouija Board and in the Hilda's Witch Haunt building. The hutch was also hand-crafted, with wood beads placed in the drawers for the knobs and feet. The colors and textures all work together in this fabulous vignette!

display/photos by Randy Vollett

*- Change Out
the Colors for a
Different Look & Feel! -*

**Changing the colors and lighting
of the garland around a display
alters the entire appearance.**

display/photos by Ray Bukovszky

The DV*All Hallow's Eve* series buildings on page 146 is set on a construction tube. Ray Bukovszky designed the vignette to be high enough for comfortable viewing, and it has space in the interior for all the boxes, so it is self contained. The fenced area of the display can be opened to get to the electrical. It is displayed year around, but by changing the garlands around the tube, it can go from an All Hallow's Eve (autumn / October - Halloween) display adorned in gold, orange and red leaves, to an All Hallow's Day (November 1 - with snow) display. Remove the snow for later Spring and Summer.

- Expand Space As Needed For Growth -

As the train grows, so does the display. An extension on the right side is added each year to accommodate the new car. John Michael Sanders painted the backdrop. display/photo by Charlie Myers

An interesting shaped brown metal étagère was painted black, with some of the brown - representing rust - retained. Grimsley Manor was placed on a shelf with a black candelabra, black candle, small skeleton, black ribbon and spider webbing. Switch out the buildings, add more Halloween related objects like spiders, chains and fence for variety!

display/photos by Leigh Gieringer

- Let No Space be Left Unused.
Any Flat Space can be Villagified -*

As new pieces are introduced into sub-series, those buildings can be separated into their own grouping. The western themed Halloween buildings sit on top of a china cabinet. Let no space be left unused! display/photo by Charlie Myers

What can be done when new pieces are being introduced into a series like the annual train cars in Halloween and now presumably with the new North Pole train. In a normal display, just build the track area longer, similar to how Charlie Myers did on page 147. Each year, the tunnel gets pushed further back into the room, since the location on the left side of the display is pre-determined. In a stylistic display, some of the cars can be placed on their own track as if they are disconnected in a freight yard. They can be set in the background or split into more than one display. Shucks, maybe they might need another engine to pull those extra cars?

The western ghost town - set on top of a china cabinet above - offers an entirely new opportunity to create. Old western antiques such as wagon wheels, cowboy boots, spurs, saddles or any old western Americana memorabilia can be added to make a dynamic vignette. Antique or thrift stores should have numerous props. Put some of those annual train car introductions into this setting, too!

*Definition not in Webster. Only a village collector would understand that any flat surface can be utilized to display their pieces.

Richard Puckett, Jr. used a fall placemat for the base of this simple to create display featuring the Dickens' Village Mordecai Mould Undertaker, Horse Drawn Hearse, and Under the Bumbershoot. Fencing, fall trees, and 12 crypt pieces were used to frame the cemetery. Small wood chips were used to make the pathway. display/photo by Richard Puckett, Jr.

"How to have a Halloween Village without Halloween Houses". Joe Meyers' Victoria Station is haunted! Other non-Halloween houses can be similarly converted. Joe hot glued moss to the building to make it look scary. Four violet spotlights from LeMax® were focused on the trees to bring out the cotton wrapped nutcrackers hanging from the trees, forming ghost-like figures. This is the same box frame on page 52. display/photo by Joe Meyers

While Department 56® had their original showroom in Eden Praire, Minnesota, they had several rooms in their "Museum" show-casing all the village products bearing their name. One of the displays is shown above. The interesting feature created by one of their designers was the gray/black styrofoam extending over the shelf and dropping toward the shelf below. The technique not only provides more space for displaying, but the effect is out-standing. Display used with permission.

display - Department 56/photo by Leigh Gieringer

display/photos by Anne Saxe

ABOVE: The beauty of having a mantle is that it is easily changed as desired. For Halloween, Anne Saxe used the same space as was featured in her display featured on pages 54-55. The buildings now include SV's Grimsley's Oddities, the RR Water Tower, a large D56 tree, Frankenstein's Windmill, three Railroad cars, the Railroad Station and RIP Tombstones. The giant black moonface on the wall adds an interesting touch. LEFT: Anne used the flat surface within the split linen closet to fit three buildings. It changes throughout the year, but in the fall, she displays her LeMax® western-themed village featuring the Dry Gulch Jail, a Mansion and stagecoach, plus many figures and desert landscaping. The similarly colored lantern adds height and is a clever addition.

Several Department 56® Halloween trees accessorized this vignette. It uses black and moss green "Freaky Fabric" pieces laid over the styrofoam and under the accessory piece respectively. Once the materials were gathered, it took about an hour to assemble.

display/photos by Pam Orman

Pam Orman used a copper-colored galvanized bucket for the base *(15" long x 11" wide x 7" deep)*. Styrofoam was cut to fit snugly which was lowered about two inches. A material called "Freaky Fabric" was used to cover the styrofoam base. The SV *Halloween Dead Creek Mill* and the *Dead Creek Mill Delivery* pieces were featured. Since the base of the accessory was green water, Pam sculpted out some styrofoam underneath the accessory so that it would appear to be sunk down into the green water (the moss green Freaky Fabric). The ring section of plastic black and orange spiders rings were removed. Several spiders were added along with red fishing worms. Halloween moss and spider web material were scattered throughout. The cord and battery packs were covered with the black fabric. Spider webbing was draped across the front of the bucket from the handle on each side.

A large coffin was created out of large sheets of styrofoam. It appears that the bones of its inhabitant are trying to get out of the giant coffin. Other props surround the coffin. WOW!

A larger Halloween village - with several buildings and numerous accessories - is created around the bones to complete this fabulous display. display/photo by Carol Cavanaugh

Pop-out pieces (8'x4"x2") were cut to form the coffin sides. For strength, two additional pieces were added in the interior.

Wood planks were etched into the top of the coffin. Holes were cut to represent broken/distressed areas. The elaborate, fallen cross was cut and positioned into the coffin. After it was shaped, the coffin was painted.

- Coffins on a Smaller Scale Serve as a Base for a Halloween Vignette -

A smaller scaled coffin can make a pleasing space saving vignette. Also constructed out of styrofoam, design it to hold a single building; or the size can be increased to include as many buildings as desired. The shape is also reconfigured from a true rectangular.

The top of this coffin was detailed to represent wood planks. Irregular and jagged openings were cut to indicate the faux coffin was old and in disrepair. After the coffin was painted in black, and weathered with rust and gray powders, a string of lights was added. Extra cording was placed behind the interior support. For additional atmosphere, include a skeleton and giant spiders crawling out of the openings.

A 2' skeleton was placed inside with an arm falling out of the "broken" area. Behind him is a string of yellow-green lights to illuminate the interior. Most of the extra cordage is placed behind the two interior pieces to hide it. The Croak-N-Haggard Mortuary building is featured here.

display/photos by Leigh Gieringer

Leigh Gieringer

John Michael Sanders

Philip Renninger

Don Rush

Mary Jewell

REALISTIC VILLAGE VIGNETTES

is Volume I of the Village Vignettes book series. It features favorite village pieces in realistic settings, with instructions on developing the techniques used. Some are stand alone vignettes, or created in special

Sneak Peek!
Realistic Village Vignettes

Leigh Gieringer

Monique Pol

John Michael Sanders

Leigh Gieringer

containers, while others are built in book cases or on shelves. Ideas presented can also be incorporated as focal points within much larger displays. These are only a few of the vignettes featured in this informative resource for village collectors.

Contributors to
Stylistic Village Vignettes
(Volume II of the Vignette Series)

Barbara Benjamin, *Arkansas Villagers*, Arkansas
    1, 76, 77, 102, 103
Bob Bogart, *Heritage Treasures of Long Island,* New York
    108. 109, 110, 111, 112, 113, 126, 127, 128, 129
Ray Bukovszky, *Southwest Villagers*, Arizona
    1, 64, 65, 97, 146, 147
Carol Cavanaugh, *Ducky 56ers*, Illimois
    155
Jeff Chretien, *Southwest Villagers*, Arizona
    72, 73, 86
Sue Chretien, *Southwest Villagers*, Arizona
    iii, 2, 9, 26, 27, 62, 72, 73, 78, 86, 92, 93, 94, 99,
    100, 106, 163
Robert & Sharon Cone, *The Village Landlords of
  South Florida*, and *Tampa Bay 56ers,* Florida
    114, 115, 119, 139
Department 56, Minnesota
    151
Mark de Vries, Netherlands
    20, 21, 68, Back Cover
Dick & Carolyn Dooley, *Queen City 56ers*, Ohio
    58, 59
Bob Eustice, *Annapolis Villagers*, Maryland
    24, 25, 129, 130
Jerry Fernon, *The Village Landlords*, Florida
    57
Gail Garbo, *Magnolia 56ers*, Mississippi
    116, 117
Leigh Gieringer, *Southwest Villagers*, Arizona
    Cover, 22, 23, 29, 30, 31, 40, 41, 44, 45, 48, 49, 53, 59,
    80, 122, 123, 124, 148, 156, 157, 163
Terry and Nancy Hellman, *Queen City Villagers,* Ohio
    81

Sue Henne, California
87
Mary Jewell, *Southwest Villagers,* Arizona
69, 95, 104, 136
Jeff & Mary Jo Lawson, *Queen City 56ers*, Kentucky
105
Frank Mapes, *Southwest Villagers*, Arizona
28, 47, 89, 131, 134, 135
Virginia Martin, *Magnolia 56ers*, Mississippi
46, 66, 67
Jeff McCann, *Queen City 56ers*, Ohio
60, 61, 138
Charles McFadden, Ohio
84
Valerie McFadden, Ohio
8, 18, 19
Mary Ellen McKenna, *Queen City 56ers*, Ohio
136
Joe Meyers, *Queen City 56ers*, Ohio
2, 52, 120, 121, 122, 150
David & Jane Morton, *BigD56ers,* Texas
73
Charlie Myers, *Southwest Villagers*, Arizona
147, 149
Susie Clough O'Brien, Ohio
10, 11, 63, 101
Pam Orman, *Magnolia 56ers*, Mississippi
154
Sue Paolello / Carol Moore, *Queen City 56ers*, Ohio
91
Anita Poitras, *Village Lamplighters of Quebec,*
(Montreal), Quebec
118
Monique Pol, Netherlands
16, 17, 82, 83, 132
Richard Puckett, Jr., *Magnolia 56ers*, Mississippi
1, 6, 7, 150
Philip Renninger, Pennsylvania
70

David Rineair, *Queen City 56ers*, Ohio
131
Linda Roberts, *Queen City 56ers*, Ohio
25, 50, 51, 52, 84, 90, 98, 137,
Don Rush, Montana
74, 75, 88, 133
John Michael Sanders, *Southwest Villagers*, Arizona
3, 4, 5, 12, 13, 14, 15, 32, 33, 36, 37, 80, 140, 141, 143,
Back Cover
Dawn Savage, *Arizona Village Collectors*, Arizona
38, 39
Anne Saxe, California
54, 55, 107, 152, 153
Debbie Shelgren, *California 56 Collectors*, California
34, 35, 42, 43, 78, 79, 105
Ellen Somerwill, *Queen City 56ers*, Ohio
50, 51, 52, 67, 96, 125
Barbara Westberg, *BigD56ers*, Texas
71, 85
Randy Vollett, *VCOM Village Collectors of Michigan*, Michigan
and Building New Worlds Home of Miniature Village
Enthusiasts, Virtual
2, 142, 143, 144, 145, Back Cover

Sneak Peek For *Realistic Village Vignettes*
(Volume II of the Vignette Series)   158-159

Pictured*:
Leigh Gieringer, Mary Jewell,
Monique Pol, Philip Renninger,
Don Rush, and John Michael Sanders

* Numerous other contributors are also
featured in this book.

About the Authors:

Leigh Gieringer has been collecting porcelain buildings and creating displays for over twenty years. She is a graduate of the University of Wisconsin - Madison, with a Bachelor of Science Degree in Fine Art. She channeled her education into the Graphic Arts. Display making became a creative outlet and challenge to discover new possibilities and limitations of what can be achieved. Yearly introductions and new products on the market provide an ever changing opportunity to implement new ideas and to perfect different artistic techniques.

Leigh was the Alpine Village feature article writer for *The Village Chronicle* for over ten years, and is currently writing the "On Display" articles for *Village D-Lights*. She has also contributed to *Village D-Tails Secondary Market Books*, and has been a speaker at Village Gatherings held across the country, as well as store events. She has created numerous store and home displays for personal enjoyment and for other village collectors. A listing of her available display building resources can be found on page 164. She is also the editor and publisher of the *Far West Skier's Guide* - a regional ski publication for snowsport enthusiasts.

Sue Chretien has been collecting D56 since 1989. It all started with getting three pieces for her Mom. She was never going to collect herself. But, we all know how that goes!

"I started with Dickens, with the idea that I would just do the buildings that pertained to 'A Christmas Carol', but when they took so long to some out, I went to Christmas In The City (tall, skinny buildings, and when you live in a tiny apartment, you could get a lot of real estate without having to give up a lot of real estate). Then, I started adding to Dickens again. When they came out with North Pole – I said, no way, no room. Until they came out with the Egg Nog Pub – I absolutely fell in love with that building. So that's when I started collecting the food-related buildings of North Pole. I also have a few Snow Village pieces (the wineries, and Melinda's Poinsettias and Mistletoe), and of course – Halloween – especially the Western Ghost Town buildings. Oops – forgot the Merry Makers and Winter Silhouette, and the Christmas Carol Candle Crowns."

"The Christmas before Jeff and I got married, I asked him to set up the CIC (as we were still living in a small apartment), and to see how he would react to just a portion of my collection. He loved it, which was good because I got him the Harley Davidson Service Center and Dealership for that Christmas. The City has been "his" ever since."

Sue was the "Marshal" *(translation - the head honcho)* of the western themed *Happy Trails to Arizona Gathering* held in the Phoenix area in 2011. She did an excellent job as the leader of the Gathering Posse. She is currently serving her second two-year term as Secretary of the National Council of 56 Clubs, as well as, the NCC's Club Connection Newsletter Editor. Sue is a Special Events Coordinator for the engineering school at Arizona State University.

Village Display Tips Resources
for Village Collectors

Books:

The Village Display Tips books feature basic to more advanced ideas and techniques to enhance your next village mega displays or small vignettes. Discussed are materials, layout development, composition, backgrounds, electrical, animation, water assimilation, carving styrofoam, other techniques for realistic displays, striking vignettes,and much more.

- The Original Village Display Tips
- Village Display Tips: Volume II
- More Village Display Tips
- Display Building on a Budget*
- Realistic Village Vignettes*
- Stylistic Village Vignettes*

*Available in a hard copy or as an e-book.

DVDs:

Each DVD is about an hour in length and applicable for developing beautiful displays in all villages. Techniques are built on screen for visual learning. Halloween: 101 is the most basic, and it is applicable for developing any village scene. The only difference is the coloration used in painting the rocks or landscaping; or leaving the styrofoam white.

- Village Scaping - Halloween: 101
- Village Scaping - Halloween: 102
- Village Scaping - Village Vignettes
- Village Scaping - Creating Large Displays
- Village Scaping - A Christmas Story

For a description of each, go to:

www.villagedisplaytips.com
Or, call: 480.600.6099 (Arizona)

Made in the USA
Charleston, SC
24 November 2013